B

Free Will in Machines

Essays on Intelligence and Consciousness

J G Lynn

Free Will in Machines

Essays on Intelligence and Consciousness

- second edition -

J G Lynn

Nian Press
Wilmington
2014

Nian Press

Copyright © 2006, 2008, 2011, 2014
by Nian Media Group; Nian Brands Corporation

Published by Nian Press, Wilmington, DE

All rights reserved. No part of this publication may be reproduced, stored in a retrieval system, or transmitted, in any form, or by any means, electronic, mechanical, photocopying, recording, or otherwise, without prior permission of Nian Brands Corporation.

Library of Congress Cataloging in Publication Data

ISBN 978-0692233771

1. Philosophy of Mind
2. Cognitive Science – Philosophy

Printed in the Unites States of America

Contents

Preface vii
Second Edition of the Preface ix
Essays on Language and Meaning 1
  On Meaning and Understanding 3
    References 28
  On Carnap's Statement Regarding Psychology
  in Physical Language 30
    References 43
Free Will in Machines 45
  Introduction 47
  The Problem with Free Will 51
    What does it mean to have Free Will? 51
    I'm free to do what I want, any old time. ... 52
    Who's Responsible? 54
    Are Machines Free to be Responsible? 57
    Yet to be Determined 60
    Compatibilism vs. Incompatibilism 61
    Principle of Alternative Possibilities 65
  Are You Conscious of Your Decisions? 70
    Intentionality and Decisions 70
    The Phenomenology of Consciousness 73
    Consciousness in Machines 76
    Why Build Conscious Machines? 77
    Criteria for Consciousness in Machines 79
    It's All Connected 84
  Discussion Points 88

- Methodology and Scientific Explanation... 88
- Managing Complexity - Consciousness Evolves........ 91
- Of Mithen Men 94
- Limitations on Current Computers 96
- Distributed Computing and Distributed Consciousness............ 100
- Does Determinism Rule out Free Will?... 103
- Dennett on Wegner, Wegner on Libet 104
- Unconscious Actions – The Role of Ideomotor Actions 107
- Volition 111
- Integration of the Conscious Mind and the Automatic Modules............ 114
- Cause and Effect 117
- Possible Worlds and Other Jedi Mind-Tricks 118
- James, is it really necessary? 123
- Conclusion 129
  - A Brave New Paradigm 129
  - Revised Criteria for Human-like Consciousness............ 134
  - Volition in Machines............ 135
  - Levels of Evolution – The Starter Life 143
- Closing Comment 145
- The Next Chapter 147
- References............ 151
- Index 157

Preface

I have spent the past twenty plus years working in computer science and software engineering. But before that, I was an undergraduate student in Philosophy which is where I became interested in philosophy of mind and what was later to become known as cognitive science. To me, cognitive science is the single best example of the benefits of inter-disciplinary studies. In writing these pages I have pulled research from many areas including logic and model theory, psychology and neuroscience, computer science, and of course the umbrella under which all of these are integrated, philosophy.

Considering questions about the representation of knowledge and information raises many questions about how humans process information, including questions about how we represent objects in our brain and mind, the role of emotions, and how our perceptions affect our behavior. After doing some background reading on the neurological basis for human and animal behavior I have come to believe that much of the progress currently being made in the areas of cognitive science and psychology is due to the advances in these areas. At the same time, I also believe that these advances present the largest challenges to our understanding of the way the mind works.

The field of cognitive science is an increasingly rich and diverse one that continues to draw on the involvement of many disciplines from psychology to computer science and at the same time becomes more relevant with each passing year. The subject of these essays, in particular "Free Will in Machines", is one additional piece of evidence of this and demonstrates both the benefits as well as the need for inter-disciplinary studies.

I would like to thank Susan Schneider and Jonathan Moreno for their feedback and suggestions on the majority of this work. I am also very grateful for the feedback from Gary Hatfield on the first two essays in this book.

J Lynn
August 2011

Second Edition of the Preface

This second edition was released to correct some typographical errors. In the process I made a few minor edits and added a few paragraphs. In the end, I opted to remove most of the new material and develop it into a separate book of essays. There is a brief chapter at the end of this edition, aptly named The Next Chapter, which summarizes where this next book is headed.

       J Lynn
       May 2014

Essays on Language and Meaning

These two essays were written in 2006 but never published. Although I have made minor edits, the text remains substantially unchanged.

The first essay discusses the notion of 'meaning' as it is used in philosophical discussions and is a key part of discussions on the nature of consciousness, especially in discussions on the criteria for consciousness. It includes a brief discussion of Fodor's "Language of Thought" (LOT) approach to consciousness. There has been much discussion on this approach over the past few years which makes this original version of the LOT theory obsolete. Nonetheless, it serves as a foundation for the very limited scope of this discussion.

The second essay is perhaps less interesting to all but philosophers, but I include it as it is delves into some of the minutia surrounding various historical aspects of language and psychology.

On Meaning and Understanding

In cognitive science we are often faced with questions regarding the place of the mind within the world in which the mind thinks, perceives, and acts. In the course of considering these questions we inevitably encounter the terms 'semantic and 'understanding'. This essay will survey the use of these terms within the context of several works. Underlying these terms (or perhaps vice versa) is the question "what does it mean to think?" or "what does it mean to have a mind?" In Minds, Brains, and Science Searle asks the question, "Can Computers Think?" Considering the mind within the context of a "thinking computer" provides a good stage on which to analyze these things since it helps us avoid our preconceptions and assumptions about the nature of the human mind. Searle claims that no machine can think by virtue of running a program because it has only syntax no semantics, i.e. a machine only manipulates symbols mechanistically without any meaning attached to those symbols or arrangements of symbols. This is a good place to start our investigation. I will intersperse Fodor's views on language, thought, and their connection to the world and the impact his views have on these terms. From there I will introduce Dretske's account of how we derive meaning from the representation of an object or other external entity. Lastly, I will present the connectionist account of meaning according to Smolensky. It is not the goal of this discourse to answer Searle's question or even to address all of the issues this question raises. These issues will be considered for the purpose and to the extent that they provide insight into how the use and definition of these terms affects the answer to the question "what constitutes a mind?" What is this term 'meaning' and where did it come from? As a starting point, we can attempt to capture a more traditional view of meaning with the following quote from Quine: "Empirical meaning…is what the sentences of one language and their firm translations in a completely alien language have in common." (Quine p. 70) Now Quine is clearly referring to the meaning in a natural language while we are more interested in a language of thought, so on to Searle's question.

Searle begins his expedition by asking the question "Can Computers Think?" He later refines this question to "Is instantiating or implementing the right computer program with the right inputs and outputs, sufficient for, or constitutive of, thinking?" (Searle p. 36) In laying out his investigation Searle describes the nature of the operations of a digital computer and characterizes them as symbol manipulation. This is most evident by viewing all computers as Turing machines. All digital computers are in fact reducible to, i.e. logically equivalent to, a Turing machine. This means that anything a digital computer is capable of doing can in principle be reduced to a machine which reads symbols one at a time from a tape and then, based on the machine's current state, can transition to another state and then move to the next location on the tape. At this point Searle introduces the objection, "But the symbols have no meaning; they have no semantic content; they are not about anything. They have to be specified purely in terms of their formal or syntactical structure." (p.31) So it seems that Searle's objection to saying that machines could have minds is that just having a language is not sufficient cause for a mind. This would then be the case for the formal grammars of a computer language as well as Fodor's Language of Thought (LOT). Clearly, Searle wants to allow that humans have minds. So what does thought require in addition to symbols? Searle makes several statements regarding this question; although they are perhaps a bit circular: "…the mind has more than a syntax, it has a semantics. There is more to having a mind than having formal or syntactic processes. Our internal mental states, by definition, have certain sorts of contents." And lastly, "Minds are semantical, in the sense that they have more than a formal structure, they have a content." (p.31)

So according to Searle to have a mind we must have the internal representation that makes up a thought as well as a 'content' of a mental state. Exactly what does it mean for a mental state to have content? Searle tells us quite clearly, "If my thoughts are to be *about* anything, then the strings must have a *meaning* which makes the thoughts about those things." (Searle p.31) This doesn't quite give us a definition of his use of content, but he certainly believes that content is closely tied to the connection between a thought and the referent of that thought. This sounds similar to what Fodor says about meaning. In discussing the evaluation of attitudes he says, "Hence, to say of a belief that it is true (/false) is to evaluate that belief in terms of its relation to the world." (Fodor p.11) These evaluations of belief are what Fodor calls 'semantic'. The same holds for other attitudes, i.e. desires, hunches, etc. The concepts of content and semantic evaluability are interconnected for Fodor. "If you know what the content of a belief is, then you know what it is about the world that determines the semantic evaluation of the belief; that, at a minimum, is how content and semantic evaluation connect." (p.11) Fodor describes what he calls the 'denotational' theory of meaning as follows. "For a mental entity to have content is just for it to have a denotation. (The denotation of a thought is whatever it is about the world that makes – or would make – the thought true. The denotation of a concept is whatever it is about the world that the concept does – or would – apply to.)" (Fodor p.72) Fodor comments that this theory has been widely thought to be false but that he feels is "very nearly true" especially in any way that is important to psychology or philosophy of mind.

Searle's argument relies heavily on the distinction between syntax and semantics. What exactly is the criteria for what is "mere syntax" and how do we get to "semantic content"? The difference between syntax and semantics for Searle, and therefore his use of meaning and content, are best captured by his hypothetical experiment known as the Chinese room. This experiment is intended to demonstrate that computers are not in principle capable of thought. He considers a computer program which simulates the understanding of the Chinese language, that is, the computer can accept questions in Chinese and give appropriate answers, and compares this to putting a person into a locked room and having them accept Chinese characters and pass appropriate Chinese characters back out. The subject does not speak Chinese but has become adept at using a rule book which tells you how to respond when given a particular set of characters. This allows the person in the room to appear as if he is able to converse in Chinese when in fact he has no idea what he is saying. In Searle's words, "…from the point of view of an outside observer, you behave exactly as if you understood Chinese, but all the same you don't understand a word of Chinese." (Searle p.33) What does this mean for our present investigation into the use of 'meaning', 'content', and 'semantics'? And what is the connection between these terms and the concept of 'understanding'? For Searle, "Understanding a language, or indeed, having mental states at all, involves more than just having a bunch of formal symbols. It involves having an interpretation, or a meaning attached to those symbols." (p. 33) In order to make this clearer, Searle contrasts this with asking and answering questions in English. Given the same situation, closed off in a room, you are passed questions in English that you are able to answer, such as 'What is your age?' The difference in this example according to Searle is that "you understand the questions in English because they are expressed in symbols whose meanings are known to you. … In the case of the Chinese… you attach no meaning to any of the elements." (Searle p.34)

So it seems that according to Searle, the notion of meaning, semantics, and content are to have an interpretation of a set of symbols. This fits well with the concept of semantics as defined within the domain of formal logic. Strictly speaking, many logicians reserve the term 'interpretation' for the specific use of dealing with interpretation between theories, but for our purposes here I do not believe there is any loss of precision in allowing this use. Also, it allows us to avoid the introduction of several other more technically correct terms which would do nothing to further the cause. Insofar as formal logic is concerned, it may seem that we may have a satisfactory candidate to the question of meaning, semantics, and perhaps even content. But in the context of understanding what it is to have a mind, have we truly come any closer? We may have connected symbols to meaning, content, and even semantics via the 'interpretation' of symbols, but in the context of minds and thoughts and understanding, have we addressed the question of what it means to have an interpretation? To continue along the line of Searle's parable, with a subtle nod to Mr. Ayer, what would it mean for a computer to have an interpretation? Intuitively it would seem that to say that a person has an interpretation of a symbol is to say that it is associated with something in the world: an object, a situation, or perhaps some value as in the temperature of the air. Searle attempts to constrain the use of the term 'interpretation' by challenging a common response to his Chinese room argument. Suppose we have a robot which is able to move around in the world and interact with its surroundings. Now suppose the robot picks up a hamburger and this causes the symbol for hamburger to occur in the computer (Searle actually says the symbol comes into the room, in keeping with his Chinese room story). I believe this response is meant to capture the notion of functional-role theory of mind. But what Searle says is "The causal interactions between the robot and the rest of the world are irrelevant unless those causal interactions are represented in some mind or other. But there is no way they can be if all that the so-called mind consists of is a set of purely formal, syntactic operations."(Searle p.35) Searle relies very heavily, and repeatedly, on this argument. How will we ever get any closer to the constituents that make up the mind if we cannot get beyond the problem of the syntactic-semantic distinction? Is there anything else that we might consider? Let us see if we can find enlightenment elsewhere.

Fodor points out that computers provide a solution to the problem of linking symbols and their semantic properties. "In computer design, causal role is brought into phase with content by exploiting parallelisms between syntax of a symbol and its semantics." (Fodor p.19) Fodor goes on to say that for the Representational Theory of Mind to succeed there must be mental symbols which have both semantical and syntactic properties. "Mental processes are causal sequences of transformations of mental representations." (Fodor p. 24) "If the occurrence of a thought is an episode in a mental process, then RTM is committed to the explicit representation of its content." He has even been able to come up with a catchy motto "No Intentional Causation without Representation." (Fodor p.25) In contrast to Searle's refrain, Fodor claims, "It is, however, in the nature of symbols that they have both syntactic and semantic properties." (Fodor p. 75) Exactly what is this content that is being represented and how do we identify it? Is this any closer than Searle was able to go? Fodor suggests that to determine the content of a belief, we have only to look at its functional role. In using this approach, Fodor tries to avoid appealing to epistemological or metaphysical considerations for the nature of meaning. In what Fodor calls the functional-role theory of mind he states that "Functional-role semantics says that content is constituted by function." (p.76) "In practice, then, functional-role theory comes down to the idea that causal interrelations among thoughts are determinants of their content." (p.77) Fodor believes that the theory of meaning comes together with the theory of mind. Both denotational theory and functional theory define semantics in terms of how mental states connect to the world. If this is accepted, then by demonstrating that a formally specified system can be used to implement both of these factors we must allow that the same system has meaning as well as semantic content, if we allow that a formally specified system can have mental states. But of course, by Searle's account this is precisely the question we are trying to answer. For Searle, the question of whether a system is capable of thought is answered by asking whether it is capable of content or meaning.

Up to this point Fodor strides with confidence, but functional-role semantics introduces the problem of coordinating the factors. (Fodor p.83) Fodor recognizes the difficulty with denotation raised by Quine, namely that "verification procedures connect terms with their denotations in too many ways". (Fodor p. 125) But the problem is not that these multiple concepts of a token, 'star' for example, are ambiguous. These are not multiple semantic values for 'star' but simply multiple routes, or multiple ways of making the connection between the object and the token. The semantic value of 'star' is what all of these connections, these routes, have in common. "What makes 'star' mean star is that the two are connected, not how the two are connected." (p. 126) For Fodor, the notion of a concept is that its tokenings covary with instances of that concept. "For we get meaning by quantifying over the routes from a symbol to its denotation." (p. 126)

Dretske has a different approach to the functional-role theory that addresses this problem. Dretske, like Fodor, defines meaning in terms of the relations between internal states and their external referents. Interestingly, he uses an example which shares many of the features of Searle's Chinese room, an inanimate instrument representing an external state of affairs. In his example he asks how we might figure out how an instrument represents the objects it represents. So if an instrument measures some value F (such as pressure or temperature) of an object, how do we go about determining what it currently 'says' about the F of that object? (Dretske p. 45) According to Dretske, "what an external observer needs to know to determine how a system (whether natural or artifactual) is representing an object is what its reaction to that object means, and what the reaction of a system means is what value of F the reaction is a reaction to when the instrument is functioning the way it was designed to function." (p.50) In Dretske's example of a pressure gauge, a reading of 10 psi means a pressure of 10 psi, i.e., the gauge is asserting that the object it is measuring has a pressure of 10 psi. It is interesting to note that there is no requirement that this measurement be veridical. If the gauge reads 10 psi when the actual pressure is 14 psi, the gauge may be said to be incorrect or misrepresenting the pressure, but it does not 'mean' 14 psi, it 'means' 10 psi, albeit incorrectly.

      An important distinction Dretske makes regarding meaning is that comprehending the meaning of one's own mind is different from knowing the mind of another. External observers must go through a process of determining what something means, as in his example of comparing the reading of a pressure gauge to the actual pressure of the object it is measuring. This adds another layer of representation, i.e. the representation of the observer which represents the representation found in the mind, or instrument, being observed. This representation of a representation is what Dretske calls metarepresentation. Not all representations of representations are metarepresentations; they must be "representations *as* representations." (p. 43) This is an important distinction in how Dretske conceives of introspection but turns out not to have significant bearing on the quest to understand terms such as 'meaning'. For Dretske, to assume that we must introspect, that we must observe ourselves as we would any other subject of observation, is a fallacy. When an external observer tries to determine what something means, he does not "occupy the state whose representational content is under investigation." (p.52) In other words, for an entity to have a mind which has meaning, that entity does not need to have a separate apparatus with which to adjudicate its meaning. "In a representational theory of mind, the source of first-person authority is derived from the fact that a system gets information about itself by perceiving the world." (p. 53) The Representational Thesis according to Dretske provides a way of viewing the mind and the contents of the mind. It provides a way to determine what the contents of the mind are. It provides "the source of first-person authority about the contents of the mind, about what it is we think and experience." (p. 57) Dretske does not say that there is no introspection in human thought, only that it is not necessary to rely on introspection to know what we are thinking or thinking about. "A representational approach to the mind gives a satisfying explanation of [the fact that] introspection has no phenomenology because the knowledge one gets by it is (itself) experience-less." (p. 62-63) Although human thought may include introspection, it has no epistemological bearing.

    The implication for our survey is that metarepresentation offers no solution to Searle's problem of getting from syntax to semantics. From Dretske's point of view, what would be needed to show that a computer had a mind? Dretske points out that a machine or animal lacks the appropriate concepts and connecting belief to know things. "They have the knowledge but not the understanding." (p.59) What is the difference between knowledge and understanding? A system can have a representation of something without 'knowing' that it has the representation. Dretske draws a distinction between "what we know" and "that we know". Knowing "that we know" requires conceptual embodiment. Machines, animals, and children "lack the power to give conceptual embodiment to what they are getting information about." (p. 60)

There is yet another perspective on the use of 'meaning', 'semantics', etc. This is the explanation of connectionism as seen by Smolensky, who claims that the distributed connectionist architecture is fundamentally different from the classical one. The key to this difference is that "mental representations and mental processes are *not* supported by the same formal entities – there are no 'symbols' that can do both jobs." (Smolensky p. 167) The connectionist architecture is split over two levels. According to Smolensky, the distributed connectionist models have the following two properties:

1. Interpretation can be assigned to large-scale activity patterns but not individual units.

2. The dynamics governing the interaction of individual units is sufficiently complex that the algorithm defining the interactions of individual units cannot be translated into a tractably specified algorithm for the interaction of whole patterns. (Smolensky p. 168)

The result of this characterization is that "the *syntax* ... resides strictly at the lower level while the *semantics* strictly resides at the upper level." (p. 168) This leads to the conclusion that an account cannot be provided in which the same elements of the model provide both the syntax and the semantics. It is for this reason that Smolensky claims that the distributed connectionist architecture is distinct from the classical one and not simply an implementation of it. This bears some resemblance to Dretske's account of introspection, but recall that for Dretske an added layer of representation led nowhere in the search for knowledge, meaning, and understanding. Smolensky on the other hand believes that it provides the solution to the bridge between syntax and semantics. While I doubt that Smolensky would want to conclude that connectionist networks introspect (at least not necessarily), he does seem to be saying that the upper level is a metarepresentation of the lower level. While the relations between elements at the lower level are distinct from the relations between elements at the higher level, this does not mean that one cannot influence the other. (p. 171)

This has a distinct impact on his theory of mind. "Distributed representations…entail that in the connectionist cognitive architecture, mental representations bear a fundamentally different relation to mental processes than is true in the Classical account." (p. 169) How does this affect our view of semantics and meaning? Smolensky believes that both Fodor's LOT theory and the connectionist model share the two claims that "Thoughts have composite structure" and "Mental processes are sensitive to this composite structure." (p. 169) The differences between these two models lie not in these two premises but in how they instantiate them. The connectionist position is that "distributed representations provide a description of mental states with semantically interpretable constituents..." (p. 184) The mental processes are specified by formal 'syntactic' rules while the mental states, the semantics, are defined at the higher level, the meta-level. In his summary, Smolensky states that "The resulting connectionist model of mental processing is characterized by context-sensitive constituents, approximately (but not exactly) compositional semantics, massively parallel structure-sensitive processing, statistical inference and statistical learning with structured representations." (p. 192) Smolensky's account provides for an explanation of how a mind can have semantic content and yet still be tied to formally specified symbols with syntactically specified interactions. It should be acknowledged that this formal syntactic structure is not the symbol manipulation in the classical sense, although it is within the definition of a Turing machine. This distinction is the source of much discussion regarding the "implementation vs. refinement" argument but does not warrant attention here. The goal here is only to show that it is possible to separate processes, computations, etc. into two (if not more) layers.

I have now presented the mind according to Searle, Fodor's beliefs about belief, what Dretske knows he knows, and Smolensky's answer to the ultimate question of life, the universe and everything. What conclusions might be drawn on 'meaning', 'semantics', and 'understanding'? From Searle, we surmise that a mind must have semantic content, there must be meaning associated with its internal representation. This requires that there is some connection between the representation and whatever it represents. This is Fodor's denotational theory of meaning. It simply states "here is a thought" and "here is what it denotes". Second, all of these accounts seem to agree that thought and minds require both syntax and semantics. For Searle this is an enigma; a mind is not a mind unless it has semantic content, but he never says where this content is to be found. Fodor sees no problem and seems to believe that semantic content just takes care of itself. It is by using and manipulating these symbols in relational denotation to some object, some state of affairs, some attitude, that they have meaning, that they derive their content from their use, from their functional role within the mental process. A mental process, remember, is simply a transformation or series of transformations of mental representation. Regarding any thought of a higher level of representation, Dretske tells us that this is not pertinent to knowledge or meaning, except in the case where we want to have thoughts about thoughts, as in thinking about the thoughts of another mind. And what of our own thoughts? Well, we have direct access to what they mean. Is this helpful or even pertinent to the use of 'meaning' and 'understanding'? It does raise the question of whether layers of thought, of representation, are necessary. In this Dretske and Smolensky are at odds. In Smolensky's connectionist account it is only through the separation of syntax and semantics into distinct layers that we can have both a formally specified implementation and have semantic content. In some sense, this does not seem to be contradictory to Fodor's account. The semantics, the meaning, arises from the relationship between the causal elements and the referents of the semantics, but it is not a direct relation. The individual elements at the lower level do not bear a direct one-to-one correspondence to the objects of the system's meaning, or even a one-to-many relationship. The causal relationship is from the lower level elements to the higher level elements and from the higher level elements to the objects of our thoughts. So what then is understanding? It seems that all we can say for certain is that understanding requires that we, a mind, or a computer know something. And to know something simply means that an internal representation bears some definite relation to whatever it represents. Perhaps it is simply what the two have in common.

References

Dretske, Fred (1995). <u>Naturalizing the Mind,</u> Cambridge, Mass. : MIT Press

Fodor, Jerry A. (1987). <u>Psychosemantics : The Problem of Meaning in the Philosophy of Mind</u> Cambridge, Mass. : MIT Press

Searle, John (1984). <u>Minds, Brains, and Science,</u> London : British Broadcasting

Schneider, Susan (2011). <u>The Language of Thought: A New Philosophical Direction,</u> Cambridge, Mass. : The MIT Press

Smolensky, Paul (1995). "Connectionism, Constituency, and the Language of Thought", <u>Connectionism : debates on psychological explanation, volume two,</u> edited by Cynthia Macdonald and Graham Macdonald, Cambridge , Mass. : Blackwell Publishers

Quine, W. V. (1959). 'Meaning and Translation', <u>Challenges to Empiricism</u>, H. Morick, originally published in <u>On Translation</u>. Cambridge, Mass.: Harvard College

On Carnap's Statement Regarding Psychology in Physical Language

This essay considers Carnap's statement that "Every psychological sentence refers to physical occurrences in the body of the person (or persons) in question" (Carnap 1932 p. 197). It will attempt to show what he meant by this statement and what he hoped to accomplish by setting this goal for psychology and for the sciences in general. It will then consider the justification for his claims and the implications. These views will then be compared to those of Tolman and Skinner.

Carnap's statement can be best understood as an advancement of the thesis of physicalism, which he states as "Physical language is a universal language and is inter-subjective" (p.166). Carnap believes that by adopting the physical language as the system language of all science, all science would be reduced to physics and metaphysics would cease to exist, or at least be regarded as meaningless. The sub-thesis of physicalism is that "...all sentences of psychology describe physical occurrences, namely, the physical behavior of humans and other animals" (p. 165). In order to support these statements he creates a linguistic framework in which he attempts to show the different types of languages and the types of sentences in these languages, modes of speech, types of laws, and relationship of some types to others through derivation. This essay will introduce only a few of these in order to make his position clearer. Once Carnap has laid out this framework he uses it to show that the content of all language can be categorized as either meaningful or meaningless. This then allows him to dismiss anything metaphysical and parallelism with it. In the end, Carnap claims that the laws of psychology are nothing more than instances of physical laws.

Carnap begins by developing a system of categorization for language use including types of sentences and expressions. He begins by distinguishing between *protocol language* and *system language*, which he states are of "first importance" to epistemological analyses. System sentences are the theoretical statements of a science; protocol sentences are the observation sentences. These two languages are correlated as are instances of system and protocol sentences. Verification of a system-sentence is done by deducing protocol sentences from it and comparing them with one's own protocol sentences. These deductions constitute the content or meaning of the system sentence. This is an important point for Carnap because as a logical positivist one of his underlying goals in advancing the thesis of physicalism is to be able to dismiss any pseudo-problems and its pseudo-sentences. This system of deductions he puts forth allows him to assert that "a sentence says no more than what is testable about it" (p.174). Any sentence confirming a system sentence must be derivable from a corresponding protocol sentence.

Furthermore, only physical language content can be confirmed. Therefore, sentences in non-physical languages can only be confirmed through confirmation in their corresponding physical sentences.

Carnap's belief is that the system sentences of psychology fit this model, i.e. that they are inter-translatable with physical sentences. He further claims that the protocol sentences of any specific person are translatable into sentences of the physical language, in other words any protocol sentence can be translated into a physical sentence which reflects the physical state of that specific person. Carnap believes that for any given psychological concept a definition may be constructed which allows for translation, or derivation, from physical concepts and that these definitions already underlie psychological practice (p. 167). Again, he is asserting that sentences of psychology be confirmed only through translation to and from the sentences of the physical language. Carnap makes a point of saying that he is neither restricting the domain of the sentences of psychology nor the terms it uses to construct them. He does demand however that these sentences as well as its terms are definable in terms of physical concepts and terms.

It is useful to consider what Carnap means by the term *translation*. When Carnap says a sentence is *translatable* into another he is saying that the two sentences are equivalent, i.e. there exist a set of rules by which the one can be deduced from the other and vice versa. If two system sentences P and Q are translatable, every protocol sentence which verifies P also verifies Q. The content of the two sentences is the same. These sentences may be in two different languages; in his example he refers to the hypothetical languages L1 and L2. These translation-rules are defined at the level of concepts. As an example of these translation-rules Carnap defines one expression "a" in terms of other expressions "b", "c" … and then using this definition or a series of such definitions derives one sentence from another (p.166). Based on this system of expression definition psychological concepts can be derived from physical concepts. In fact his thesis is that for every psychological concept a definition can be provided which makes it inter-translatable with a physical concept (p. 167). What he is saying then is that if this cannot be done, the psychological concept is not a valid one; it is meaningless and any sentence containing it is meaningless.

For Tolman, the emphasis on meaning in this sense is not quite as important. He takes a completely operational approach and refers to his brand of psychology as "operational behaviorism", a functionalistic version of behaviorism which predated the physicalistic behaviorism (Hatfield p. 2). What Tolman means by this is that his only interest is "…the prediction and control of behavior" (Tolman 1936 p.129). This model is achieved through what we might call a pseudo-mathematical model, representing behavior as functions whose only parameters are the "independent variables" which represent stimuli, physiological drive, heredity, training, and age(maturity). The functional relation of these variables to the presence or absence of a specific behavior is achieved strictly through experimentation. There is no consideration of the meaning of statements, only of their ability to explain and predict behavior.

Although Skinner would admit to Carnap's thesis regarding the translatability of psychological sentences into physical ones in principle, he would likely raise the concern that science must be careful not to define the concepts of psychology in terms of those of physiology without sufficient validation. He cites what he sees as a similar fallacy in the works of Holt. Skinner claims Holt criticizes the use of the term 'instinct' to explain behavior and then offers an alternative explanation which in Skinner's opinion differs only in the addition of a "neural reference … assigned to the law which is lacking for the instinct" (Skinner 1938 p. 427). The fallacy, he claims, is that there is nothing to support this reference; that is, there is no justification for defining the behavioral concept in terms of the neural concept. Skinner also believes that "Deduction and the testing of hypotheses are actually subordinate processes in a descriptive science ..." (p.437)

Carnap refutes parallelism which claims that the system sentences of psychology are distinct in terms of content from the physical sentences, that is, that the statements of psychology describe "a state of affairs not identical with the corresponding physical structure, but rather, only accompanied by it ..." (Carnap 1932 p.173). This criticism reflects Carnap's disregard for the notion of consciousness as a distinct entity and a disregard for metaphysics in general. His attitude towards metaphysics is evident from his comparison of psychology to the more mature sciences which are further along in their "decontamination from metaphysics" (p. 174). Psychology on the other hand embraces metaphysics which he says can be seen by this parallel view which relies on the postulation of consciousness as an entity separate from observable behavior and the existence of which is not empirically determinable. Carnap expounds on this line of thought in later works, asserting that such abstract entities, "linguistic expressions", are merely "ways of speech not actually designating anything" (Carnap 1956 p. 43).

    Tolman did not share Carnap's disdain for the conscious although he claimed his view was nonmetaphysical (Hatfield p. 8). For Tolman, it is necessary to describe behavior, specifically behavior-acts, in terms of purpose or what he refers to as postulations, i.e. the inference by the subject of purpose (Tolman 1926 p. 355). His explanation of behavior foreshadows intentionality, e.g. the rat who mistakenly runs into the wall because he postulates the existence of a longer corridor based on previous experience.

Certain of these postulations are what Tolman refers to as "conscious-awareness (p. 366). Carnap writes that if his thesis regarding the correlation between the different types of sentences is correct, the same derivation is possible between psychological laws and physical laws. Sentences can be distinguished as single sentences about specific occurrences and general sentences which we would typically refer to as laws. The general can be divided into two types: laws concerning specific qualities of a specific type and universal-conditional statements or causal laws. These laws or general sentences are what allow us to derive system sentences from protocol sentences in what Carnap calls rational derivation. An example of rational derivation from a protocol sentence would be to start with an observation such as 'the perception of the excitement of an individual' along with a "general sentence" or law, e.g., 'when I perceive a person to have a certain facial expression I conclude they are excited'. From this we conclude a system sentence such as 'Mr. A is now excited'. Carnap also acknowledges the intuitive method of derivation. This is similar to rational derivation except that the system sentence is obtained without the general law(s) but immediately from the protocol sentence. Carnap refers to this as immediate perception. Occasionally a system sentence may need to be retracted in the face of contradictory protocol sentences, but this does not detract from his system. It is simply a matter of reasoning from a false premise. In describing this methodology, Carnap is trying to make psychology fit the model of the physical sciences and goes so far as to say that psychological laws are just special cases of physical laws (Carnap 1932 p. 167).

Skinner also believes that we will eventually see a unification of the sciences including psychology and physiology and admits that it is a positive advancement of the sciences "when terms at one level of analysis are defined ("explained") at a lower level" (Skinner 1938 p.

428). He even goes so far as to state the "statement of all knowledge in a single 'language'" is one of the objectives of science (p. 429). But he also warns against tying the progress of one branch of science to that of another for fear of the one hindering the other. Skinner contends that the behavior and nervous system must remain two independent subjects of research. He would say that by keeping the sentences of psychology (the science of behavior) equivalent to physical sentences, of neurology for example, the development of psychology would be limited by the advances in neurology. He does admit however that data about the physical system by itself will establish or strengthen hypotheses or theories about behavior (p. 423). While behavior is often explained in terms of what he calls "neural correlates" it is usually only possible where the meaning of the explanation is simple (p. 425). He points out in the same paragraph that the two sciences have demonstrated some success in explaining one in the terms of another only because only simple concepts have been addressed.

Carnap's thesis is an attempt to very thoroughly and systematically unify the epistemological world. It is an attempt to make physical language the universal language to which all of science must conform. In doing so he hopes to rid the world of metaphysics and meaningless statements void of content. In Tolman's essay 'A Behavioristic Theory of Ideas' in his closing remarks he concedes that his treatment of consciousness is "hopelessly chaotic and superficial" (Tolman 1926 p. 369). On this point he and Carnap would surely agree.

References

Carnap, R (1932). 'Psychologie in physikalischer Sprache', Erkenntnis 3:107-42. Trans. 1959 G. Schick, 'Psychology in Physical Language', in A. J. Ayer (ea.), Logical Positivism, New York: Free Press, 165-97.

Carnap, R (1956). 'Empiricism, Semantics, and Ontology', Challenges to Empiricism, H. Morick, originally published in Meaning and Necessity. Chicago: University of Chicago Press

Hatfield, G. (), Behaviorism and Naturalism, Cambridge History of Philosophy, Cambridge University Press

Skinner, B. F. (1938). Behavior of Organisms: An Experimental Analysis, New York: Appleton-Century.

Skinner, B.F. (1950). 'Are Theories of Learning Necessary?', originally published in Psychological Review 57:193-216

Tolman, E. C. (1926). 'A Behavioristic Theory of Ideas', Psychological Review 33:352-69.

Tolman, E. C. (1936,1951). <u>Collected Papers in Psychology</u>, University of California Press, 115-129

Free Will in Machines

-Volition and Consciousness-

Introduction

Most of us believe we have free will. We believe that to the extent allowed by our circumstances, we each choose what we do, what we say, and what we think. This notion of freedom carries along with it the implication of personal responsibility for those actions. By being free to make our own decisions, we assume at least some responsibility for the consequences of those decisions. Is it possible for a machine to have this same free will? Are machines capable of achieving the prerequisite level of consciousness to be held accountable for their own actions? In science fiction from Asimov's "I, Robot" to the more recent "Terminator" we have been warned of the evils of unbridled technology and its potential for the ultimate destruction of mankind. Is what governs our behavior any different than what governs the behavior of a machine? Once the exclusive province of fantasy and fiction, neuroscience has shown the cause of "good" vs. "bad" behavior to be tied to specific brain systems. As our understanding grows of this connection between mind and body, our legal and ethics theories regarding moral responsibility will need to adapt, perhaps to include machines.

By the time we entered the twentieth century western philosophy was firmly entrenched in dualism, the notion that mind and body are composed of two different types of "stuff"; mind is not composed of matter. This view leads to the conclusion we are made of two substances that cannot cause a change in the other: the mind-body problem. Gilbert Ryle refuted this problem by asserting that this distinction between mind and body as substantially different was flawed. Ryle referred to this view of cooperative interactions between material and non-material stuff as the "ghost in the machine" (Ryle p15). This separation of mind and body reflects the common sense view still held by many people today. Recent advances in neuroscience are challenging these long held dualist views. No longer confined to academic discussion among philosophers, this topic is rapidly becoming relevant in both the professional and lay arenas, the medical and legal fields in particular. Any challenge to the status quo of our current belief structure would raise serious issues that would have far reaching implications for our modern legal systems as well as many religions of the world.

In this paper I will show that contrary to our intuitions and preconceptions, there is nothing known to us today that precludes the possibility that machines have the ability both to think and to make decisions of their own free will. While science does not yet provide us with sufficient knowledge to completely understand fully the nature of consciousness, there is nothing in what we do understand of the mind that will not be reproducible in machines. There is also no evidence that anything associated with the way humans make decisions *of their own free will* cannot also be implemented in a machine. While there are certainly technological challenges to be met, perhaps more difficult than we could imagine, there should be no difference in principle between these implementations in machines and those in the human brain.

I will begin by establishing a perspective on free will issues including that of responsibility, the question of living in a deterministic universe and the consequences to the free will question. I will then turn to the bearing that consciousness has on the free will question along with the role that intent plays in consciousness and free will. I will then briefly describe some of the current work in machine consciousness and take an initial look at possible criteria for determining whether a machine is conscious, and some arguments for and against the possibility of machine consciousness. What are the necessary and sufficient conditions for a person to possess consciousness? Do the same conditions for consciousness in humans hold for machines?

I will then comment on the need to adopt a methodology that will allow the unification of the cognitive science community and allow progress toward a more complete understanding of the human mind. From here I will discuss one hypothesis of how the development of a highly evolved system can account for what we call free will, and demonstrate that any limitations in the computer today are due only to a lack of the same level of development. From here I present a few points of contention in the evolution hypothesis and where possible some counterpoints.

I will then summarize what I believe to be the knowns and the unknowns in the quest for understanding the nature of our own minds and the possibility that in the future we may share some of those characteristics with machines. There is much yet to be discovered, but based on what science has dissected so far there is nothing that humans can do that machines will not be able to. In fact, most things they will probably do better.

The Problem with Free Will

What does it mean to have Free Will?

For centuries people have speculated about just how free we really are to control our own destiny. Early on these discussions centered on considerations of a religious or spiritual nature; but as the scientific community evolved, questions about free will become more and more analytical and as the field of psychology emerged the questions became even more pointed. Behaviorism for example gave rise to the "nature vs. nurture" question. And as we try to explain more and more of our world in terms of the physical laws that govern it, we struggle to apply the principles of biology, sociology, psychology, and neuroscience to questions about the extent to which we are truly responsible for our own fate. Does mental capacity affect whether or not someone can be held responsible for their own actions? Can an otherwise average person be held responsible for their decisions under extreme circumstances such as illness or the trauma of a crisis? We live in a world in which we are led to believe that in the near future we will be able to explain, if not predict, every minute detail of the physical world around us. In such a world what room is left for the human will? It is easy to find ourselves wondering if it is even meaningful to speak of a person acting of their own free will. To understand what it means to have free will and what problems arise when we try to define it we begin by considering free will within the context of freedom.

I'm free to do what I want, any old time.

Discussions of freedom are ubiquitous in today's world and the concept of freedom is central to the notions of volition and free will. Exactly what does it mean to "have freedom" or to "be free"? A simple answer is to say that we are free if we are able to choose as we wish. We choose what to say, where to go, what to eat, and what to think. Much of the time, this is what people mean when they speak of freedom. When we speak of freedom in this way, we are asserting that we are free to make choices without the imposition of constraints by external forces. When we make choices without the interference of others we say that these choices are made *of our own free will*. But what is the connection between our personal freedom and our free will? Are they the same thing? Does one entail the other? Is free will a necessary condition of freedom – or vice versa?

We might describe free will by saying that for free will to exist there must exist the possibility for a person presented with a choice between two (or more) actions to "freely" choose one of those actions. To remove some of the ambiguity, we can add the condition that the two choices must be possible. This eliminates a certain type of case frequently encountered in philosophical circles such as the following: "given a *choice* between leaping fifty feet into the air and remaining on the ground, can a person be said to 'choose' not to leap fifty feet into the air?" After all, since no person could actually have leapt fifty feet into the air, choosing not to do so doesn't seem like much of a decision. For it to count as a *real* choice, it has to be possible for the person has to have actually chosen either. The person has to have had the power, or ability, to perform the action and the ability to have done otherwise. This prerequisite of *possibility* occurs in several approaches to the free will question. One such approach to describing free will is referred to (and refuted) by Harry Frankfurt as the Principle of Alternative Possibilities (PAP). PAP asserts that persons are only responsible for what they have done if they could have done otherwise (Frankfurt p5). Before considering this principle in more detail we should look at another key concept in the question of free will – responsibility.

Who's Responsible?

When we consider questions about whether a person has made a choice of their own free will, often we are considering the underlying question regarding their accountability for their actions. We want to know who's responsible – who's to blame? In our day to day life we are aware that we will be held accountable at our jobs, we are responsible for our children, and we are held responsible for our mistakes. Most of us accept this because we accept the premise that we make decisions of our own free will. If I am told to pay a fine for driving through a red light, it is because the police, the courts, and I are in agreement that I chose to drive through the intersection despite the fact that the light was red. But it is not always simple to bring everyone into agreement when it comes to assignment of blame. Take for example a case where there are several causes that contribute to the end result. If I leave my coffee pot on and it starts a fire – whose fault could it be but my own? But if it turns out that the fire was started due to some defect of the manufacturer it then becomes the fault of the manufacturer – doesn't it? Or perhaps the spark that precipitated the fire was brought on by a leaky pipe due to a poor repair job done by a plumber hired by my landlord because he was the cheapest plumber he could find. Now we have four different parties that seem to be responsible in one way or another for the fire. Who's to blame? Who *caused* the fire? This same complexity that seems to take assignment of blame from obvious to debatable is the problem we encounter in asking questions about "Did *I* decide to …?"

When we speak of assigning responsibility in the above example, we are considering how multiple contributors may have caused some end result – the fire. But we don't actually consider whether the landlord, the plumber, or the manufacturer contributed to my decision (or lack thereof) to turn off the coffee pot. In this case, the faults are *external* to me. I am using the terms *external* and *internal* relative to where the effect lies. The actions of the landlord and the plumber are *external* in the sense that the events all have an effect on the end result but do not influence anything I myself did. An example of an action with an internal effect would be if I found out that someone was secretly drugging me by putting a hallucinogen in my Wheaties. Here we have an external agent acting on me in a way that alters my thinking and therefore affecting my decision making ability. The immediate effect of the hallucinogen is to alter my thought processes, which is internal to me. This is the classic "I wasn't myself" defense. How can we hold someone responsible for their actions if some external force *caused* them to behave differently?

    The courts are full of cases where a person is accused of some wrongful action but holds that their responsibility is mitigated by other circumstances. Someone shoots a person but claims their actions were necessary to protect his family. Could the person have done otherwise? In some sense it was necessary for the person to act as they did. This brings us back to the phrase "could have done otherwise." It turns out that the way we interpret this phrase will to a large extent determine the conclusion we ultimately draw regarding the free will question. In fact, it is *responsibility* that allows us to set *free will* apart from *freedom* in general. It is this idea of *responsibility* that distinguishes *free will* as something that we control whereas *freedom* is a state that we enjoy.

Are Machines Free to be Responsible?

When we ask whether machines are capable of volition, we are asking what controls their actions. Volition, or will, is the part of human thought that makes decisions and commits them to action. Can machines share this characteristic with the human mind? We might begin by asking these two key questions: Can a machine be free? Can a machine be responsible? Just what does it mean for a machine to be free? We could revert back to the definition "free from external constraints". A machine is free if it is able to do whatever it chooses. But in this sense of freedom, machines which are free might include battery operated toys. As long as I don't "kill" it by turning it off or removing its batteries, it is free to run around the living room floor, bumping into furniture and bouncing off of walls. It is unconstrained in the same sense that we like to believe we are: constrained only by the physical limits of the world in which we live. But this type of freedom seems somewhat trivial. Most of us would like to believe that there is a difference between the freedom ascribed to a child's toy and the freedom that we enjoy. And it certainly doesn't seem that we would want to say that a simple toy is responsible for its own actions. Consider this scenario. If I throw a baseball and it breaks a window, I might claim that I didn't break the window, the baseball did. But most of us would want to say that although the baseball was the proximate cause, *I* was the reason the baseball went through the window. This again brings up the question of cause and effect. We will need to dig into the question of cause in more detail. But it also brings up a new issue – that of intent. In some cases we claim that for someone to be held responsible for an act we must believe that they intended for the outcome to be as it was – otherwise we call it an accident. We will return to the role intention plays in decisions and responsibility, but for now let's just say that freedom and responsibility entail that one's actions are controlled by themselves and that their actions caused the intended outcome.

So what would it take to convince us that a machine had just as much freedom as we do? It seems that we would want to have a set of criteria that would apply to both humans and machines alike. For that matter, if we want to be completely unbiased we would probably want to claim that our criteria would apply equally to anyone or anything we want to consider – animals, aliens, etc. – so we will refer to these various things as *agents*. We can offer the following proposed criteria:

> *An agent is free, in a meaningful sense, if and only if it can act according to its own decisions and under its own control.*
>
> *An agent is responsible for its actions if and only if it acts according to its own intentions.*

The above criteria seem self-evident, yet there is a nagging feeling that we have simply displaced the problem to the question of what we mean when we say *its own decisions* and *under its own control.* We will also need to address the question of what we mean by *intention*, especially as it applies to machines. As we saw above, there are often many contributing causes to any outcome, some of which are external in nature and some which are internal. To the extent that these causes affect the internal state of the agent making a decision to act, it would seem that the degree of freedom and responsibility an agent possesses may be determined by external factors.

Yet to be Determined

On the one hand we want to believe that we control our own destiny, that we are the cause of our own behavior, yet on the other hand we believe that every action has a cause. The closer we look at any chain of events, and the causes of the events, the more it seems that events are ultimately caused by factors outside of our control. The more we understand about the world around us the more we find that these events, our decisions and our actions, are determined with the same certainty of the rest of the physical laws that govern our universe. This would seem to leave little room for free will. In what sense can we say that we as thinking, willful beings make a decision between one choice and another, when every series of events is determined by the unchanging, unbreakable physical laws of the universe?

The belief in *determinism*, often referred to as the doctrine of necessity, holds that all events derive from their necessary and sufficient causes according to the physical laws of the universe. Here is how Dennett defines determinism:

> "A universe is *deterministic* if there are transition rules (the laws of physics) that *determine exactly* which state description follows any particular state description. If there is any slack or uncertainty, the universe is indeterministic."
> (Dennett 2003 p28)

The consequence of living in a deterministic universe is that anything that takes place is inevitable. In other words, whatever occurs could not have been otherwise. Traditional philosophical views hold that living in a deterministic universe would rule out free will and the principle of alternate possibilities would seem to support this.

Compatibilism vs. Incompatibilism

More recently a position known as *compatibilism* has reemerged that claims there is no contradiction between the propositions that "the will is caused" and "we have free will". This stance dates back as far as the Stoics of ancient Greece but has seen a resurgence in the writings of Wegner, Libet, and Dennett.

Classical compatibilists such as Hobbes view freedom as the absence of constraints.

Hobbes characterizes this freedom as a man who "finds no stop, in doing what he has the will, desire, or inclination to do" (Hobbes p159). The focus is on external constraints rather than constraints internal to the self. He finds that "Liberty, and necessity are consistent: …because every act of man's will, and every desire, and inclination proceedeth from some cause, and that from another cause, in a continual chain, whose first link is in the hand of God the first of all causes, proceed from *necessity*" (Hobbes p160). The compatibilist approach often has a subjunctive element, allowing that one could or would do otherwise *if* they had wanted to, even if in fact what they did want to do was determined.

Those that believe that free will and determinism are in conflict are known as *incompatibilists*. Those such as Carl Ginet go so far as to say that "the concept of a decision makes it impossible that any event be both identified as a decision and said to be caused" (Ginet1962 p55). One of the most widely used arguments for incompatibilism is Ginet's Consequence Argument (CA) summarized here (Ginet1990 p106):

> Assume determinism is true; then our acts are all the consequences of events of the past and the physical laws of nature. Since we control neither the laws of nature nor

the events of the past (especially those before we were born), we do not control our own actions.

At first glance, this appears to be a rather solid argument. Incompatibilists are left to draw one of two conclusions. Either free will does not exist or determinism is false. Those who believe that free will exists and that determinism is false are called *libertarians*. In denying determinism, libertarians are faced with the premise that events, or at least some events, are without cause. This *indeterminism* is difficult to reconcile with the belief in free will and responsibility. Events which are undetermined (quantum jumps in atoms are an oft-cited example) are completely by chance. But if our own actions are by chance, how responsible can we be for them? Some such theories attempt to reconcile this by introducing extraphysical causes or *agents of cause* (Kane p48). Though it may seem that providing some extra factor which intervenes in the series of causes addresses the question of infinite regress, we have only moved the train to a different track. Any agent capable of influencing our actions must itself have a cause for certainly it is subject to the same physical laws as we are. To avoid the same problem with an infinite series of agent-causings that are random or undetermined, the agent-causalists claim "the agent-causal relation is unique and cannot be treated like any other event or occurrence. ... Immanent agent-causation is not the sort of thing that can in principle occur randomly or by chance, any more than it can be caused" (Kane p50). This is appealing and it avoids the problems of infinite regress, but it moves the theory outside of the laws of nature. If the events of an agent of cause are not subject to the laws of causation, how could such a non-physical entity influence our mind and body? We are headed right back into the trap of dualism.

Often those who refute CA focus on what it means to control our own actions. One way to interpret this is to make "controlling our own actions" equivalent to the question of what we "can or cannot do" or to put it another way, whether we "could have done otherwise."

So while CA and PAP may seem to be contradictory, much of the contention rests on how we define and what we believe about this notion of "could have done otherwise" so we should return to some of the arguments for and against PAP.

Principle of Alternative Possibilities

We saw that according to Frankfurt's Principle of Alternative Possibilities, a person can only be responsible for their actions if they had the power to do otherwise. So PAP requires responsibility as a precondition of free will and the possibility of doing otherwise as a precondition of responsibility. It follows that having *viable options* is a precondition of free will. To put it simply – no options – no decision – no responsibility – no free will. If volition is required for responsibility, then the power to do otherwise would be a necessary precondition of volition.

When Martin Luther seceded from the Roman Catholic Church he is quoted as saying "Here I stand. I can do no other" (Frankfurt p86). The claim can be made that this should be interpreted as meaning it would have been impossible for him to have done otherwise. In other words, in a determinist world, by that point in his life all of the events (the effects of causes) had brought him to a point where he literally could not have done otherwise even if he had wanted to, and by some interpretations he could not have even 'wanted' otherwise. "It is clear, of course, that the impossibility to which Luther referred was a matter neither of logical nor of causal necessity. ... What he was unable to muster was not the *power* to forbear, but the *will*" (Frankfurt p86). Taking this view to the extreme would mean that (according to PAP) Luther could not to be held responsible for his actions. But what we want to say is that Luther, like everyone else, is responsible for his actions.

If we view the Luther example under the determinist view, the problem we encounter is that for Luther to be responsible for his action, at least some of his earlier choices must have been of his own doing – there must have been a choice between two possible alternatives. But if we attempt to identify some key point in his past where we can say, "Aha! Here is the decision that caused Luther to think in this way; and here is another!" then we will never find anything useful. From this, one might conclude that PAP must be false.

Ginet finds the so-called Luther argument unconvincing because Frankfurt interprets PAP incorrectly. He refutes this and another group of examples commonly referred to as Frankfurt-type examples which attempt to refute the requirement for alternative possibilities in the existence of free will. Ginet begins by restating PAP as it applies to actions:

> "S is responsible for its being the case that S acted in a certain way at a certain time only if S could have made it not the case that S acted in that way then" (Ginet1996 p404).

The general scenario in the Frankfurt-type examples is that our subject, Jones, is making up his mind whether or not to do something. A second person, Dr. Smith, has the ability to control Jones's actions (typically though some drug or neuron-manipulation) but wants to avoid intervening unless necessary. If Jones chooses to act according to Dr. Smith's wishes, no intervention is necessary and Jones acted completely of his own free will. Yet there was no possibility of Jones deciding otherwise, since had he attempted to do so, Dr. Smith would have intervened in time and Jones would have acted according to Dr. Smith's wishes anyway. There are many variations and counterexamples of the Frankfurt-type. The key thing to note is that Jones cannot do otherwise because Dr. Smith will not let him. Although this argument may seem problematic to PAP, if we modify the prerequisite to "the possibility to do otherwise when given the opportunity" we can avoid this pitfall. In the above example Jones could not have done otherwise, but only because Smith would not have allowed Jones that opportunity. That lack of opportunity is not due to a lack of will on the part of Jones, it is a physical constraint.

Again, we have only displaced the issue by moving the variable in question from one place to another; this is a valuable step to take. It removes the uncertainty from the subject (e.g. Jones) and places it "out there" in the world. The question is no longer so much whether or not we are in control of our thoughts as it is do we live in a universe where the laws of physics are deceptive and our mind is subject to unknowable laws of metaphysics. The objections raised by the Frankfurt examples make free will dependent on the subject being aware of what the true possibilities are. They attempt to show that the subject is not free to choose, but what they really demonstrate is that the subject does not necessarily know what the limits of the world are. He is not aware of all of the physical constraints to which he is subject. It is common in everyday life that a person makes a choice where the end result could have not been otherwise, yet this does not necessarily relieve them from responsibility, or at least leaves them accountable for their intentions. Consider the example of attempted murder.

Both the Luther example and the Frankfurt-type examples run into a problem with original cause. As long as we see things in a classical determinist light, any event will leave us with an unanswered question regarding the cause of that event. As we inquire about the responsibility for an action, the responsibility will always lead us backward to the previous cause. As we saw above with the libertarian agent-causation approach, any attempt to avoid this infinite regress by introducing factors not subject to the rigid laws of causation ultimately yield theories that rely on metaphysical uncertainty and mystery and therefore outside the realm of and scientific discourse or verification.

Are You Conscious of Your Decisions?

In order to understand the nature of volition and decisions, it is necessary to have some understanding of the context in which these activities take place. It may seem prima facie evident that for a person to make decisions they need to be conscious. Likewise, if we assert that any being, animal or machine, is capable of making decisions of its own free will, it would seem natural to presuppose consciousness.

Intentionality and Decisions

Intentionality is a class of terms such as 'believe', 'expect', 'desire', and of course 'intend'. What all of these terms share is the fact that they each take an object of intent. They all presuppose a mental state in which an attitude is directed toward some object. When we say "I believe it is raining" our attitude is directed toward the state of our environment as 'is raining'. When we say "I intend to go to sleep soon" we are asserting a future state of affairs. In the first example, we are simply making a claim regarding the true and accurate state of the world at some point of time. In the second example, the same is true but with the added aspect that we are announcing our decision to go to sleep. As the agent which is a key factor in our future state we are not only predicting the future, we are causing it to occur (assuming we can go to sleep whenever we choose). When speaking of intentionality in such an intuitive manner, there seems to be no reason to call into question whether having a mind is a necessary condition of intentionality. We will see later, that some explanations of intentionality do not require this.

    Speaking non-technically, it seems obvious that making a decision entails intending to do so. Most people would agree that the process of forming an intention is a part of the process of making a decision. James Hall offers a specific case of deciding in which forming an intention is not simply a process leading up to decision but sometimes *is* the decision. The common view is that "deciding consists in forming an intention to do something as a result of deliberating" (Hall p553). Seeing that deciding commits us to actions we also observe that intention may do so as well, although perhaps not as strongly. This view extends the role of intention from that of an internal mental state related to formulating a decision to the role of committing to that decision. When we are deliberating over two choices, the point at which we can be said to have reached a decision is sometimes the point that we have reached a strong intention. If I say "I intend to go to New York tomorrow" I have not only informed you of my thoughts, I have informed you of my decision to perform some action. By saying this to you I have to some extent committed to you that I will be in New York tomorrow. This could be considered what is known as a *performative utterance* (Austen p32). The intention is not just part of the process; it is part of the result. Sometimes this is the result of choosing between two conflicting intentions. Perhaps I have intentions of getting some things done that would preclude me from going to New York. Hall summarizes that "deciding could be forming an intention as a result of deliberation in those cases where the decision is between previously formed intentions" (Hall1978 p563). Not only have I reached a certain point of certainty by announcing the results of my deliberation, but if announcing my decision to you has an effect on your actions, I may have also incurred some responsibility to follow through on those intentions. If you were planning to go to New York for the sole purpose of meeting me there, my utterance is an agreement, even a contract of sorts, to do so. "So even though we may not wish to go so far as to classify the commitment to action that comes through deciding, as a moral responsibility per se, it nevertheless plays an important role in everyday life. A society in which people could not expect themselves or others to implement the decisions they make would be an even less perfect society than ours presently is" (Hall1978 p563).

Since action is a key part of any criterion for free will and decision a key part of action, it is important to be clear regarding the role of intention in decision. Ultimately, the only consequence this distinction appears to have for the free will question is that there is not a clear dichotomy between intentions and decisions as we might have thought.

The Phenomenology of Consciousness

Many philosophers and perhaps some psychologists are dedicating all of their brain power to better understand the true nature of the phenomenon of conscious coined *qualia*. This has become known as "The Hard Problem of Consciousness", coined by David Chalmers and has various characterizations, all of which revolve around the existence and nature of experience and subjectivity (Chalmers p226). It is a "hard problem" because any attempt to account for this part of consciousness has become a quagmire of explanation. The term *qualia* itself is somewhat elusive, typically defined as the features of perception and bodily sensations which contain information not accounted for in physical data such as nerve impulses (Chalmers p226). Among the properties of qualia are their private nature, i.e. there cannot be any meaningful comparison between persons, and in fact they can only be apprehended by direct experience.

    Arguments regarding consciousness that rest on any such phenomenological status are problematic. Any scientific investigation must rely exclusively on subjective accounts. For example, if events and experiences that are not conscious are categorized as non-phenomenal, how would we account for those that occur in a dreaming state? We have all had dreams that were vivid enough to defy differentiation between the experiences of our dream world and the real.

    To assert that in addition to all of the collective states of our brain and related systems there is some other *stuff*, whatever it may be, is to commit what Gilbert Ryle called a *category mistake*, a misunderstanding of the nature of certain terms (Ryle p17). The collection of nerve impulses and electrochemical states of our thinking machinery *is* the experience. To look for a separate, additional component over and above the components of the experience is a misunderstanding – an incorrect view. Consider the analogy of a well-maintained car. We say it is good shape. The wheels, the engine, the transmission, the suspension, etc. are all in perfect working order and well-tuned. The car is in great shape, but I can't seem to find its *shape*. Where can I look to see if this is a good shape or a bad shape? Surely we have the technology to measure quantitatively what the condition of the car is. We should be able to devise some instrument that could be applied to the car to measure the shape. But there is no such instrument because we have already measured everything there is to measure in the engine, the transmission, etc. There is no quality that exists in and of itself; there is only the concept of a well-tuned car which performs well.

    Although much has been written regarding qualia and the phenomenological aspect of the mind, until we have figured out how to account for the subjective impressions in some empirical measure, it is difficult to include them in any scientific discussion on consciousness. I cannot see how anything useful can come of any further research and investigation on qualia or of any phenomenology of consciousness in general until a basis has been established in one of the underlying sciences such as biology, neuroscience or physics.

Consciousness in Machines

To better understand what "being conscious" would mean for a machine, some researchers are designing models which mimic, duplicate, or approximate human consciousness. This type of work, known collectively as machine modeling of consciousness or MMC, is a combination of science and engineering – integrating the analytical research from biology, psychology, and neuroscience with the disciplines of computer science, applied mathematics, and process engineering.

MMC researchers such as Igor Aleksandar believe that the attempt to create a conscious machine is quite distinct from the now familiar endeavor of the 1960s, 70s, and 80s known as Artificial Intelligence or AI. Whereas AI focused on solving complex and difficult problems that mimicked the results of human intelligence, MMC is interested in the mental states of the machine; "…the modeling fits the appellative if and only if it addresses the mental state of a machine as an explicit, symbolic model of the world with the machine computation explicitly represented within it (the functional stance) or if it addresses mechanisms that materially are capable of such representation in a cellular non-symbolic way (the material stance)" (Aleksander2007 p87).

Approaches to MMC differ in several ways. The most distinctive feature is the extent to which each implementation corresponds to the mechanisms of the brain. While some attempt to mimic aspects of the human brain in the hopes of finding a similar level of success, others completely ignore this design goal. To some degree, this may reveal an underlying belief that the way the brain is organized is key to achieving consciousness. It is important to note that although some designers may choose to look at human neurology for clues as to how to design their machines, they do not suggest that these "silicon copies" are the only way to successfully duplicate consciousness.

Why Build Conscious Machines?

There are at least two reasons to build conscious machines. The main goal for Aleksander is to "clarify through synthesis the notion of what it is to be conscious." For him the goal is to build machines that are more autonomous and require less pre-programming. He describes the conscious machine as one that will be less reactive and more "contemplative" in nature. "This provides a machine with a significant opportunity for dealing with circumstances unforeseen by the programmer" (Aleksander p89).

If the goal is simply to understand consciousness, how important is it to imitate the architecture of the brain? Many researchers choose to take this approach. Is the implication that consciousness can only be achieved by adhering to one principle? Is there a key to consciousness in the architecture without which no animal or machine can ever be any more than a very powerful calculator? Not necessarily. Other than those who claim that no machine can ever be conscious, nobody asserts that the brain holds any magic ingredient that is necessary for consciousness. So what are the reasons for following the brain blueprint? I count two. First of all, we are by no means master engineers of consciousness. When trying to build something you don't understand that well, it's best to stick to the blueprint. That's the difference between an apprentice and a master. Secondly, by keeping our machine as close to ourselves as possible, it makes it simpler to run comparisons of the two.

We can look at how certain stimuli affect a certain subsystem in our brain and compare it to our synthetic counterpart. Note that this second reason does not apply to testing "in the large". For example, Rorschach tests could be performed on a machine regardless of whether it was a neurological duplicate of a brain or an assemblage of vacuum tubes.

Criteria for Consciousness in Machines

Aleksandar summarizes what he believes are some of the criteria currently applicable to MMC based on what is known about the design of existing work. No one design will necessarily meet all of the criteria, but he feels that for a machine to be considered conscious, a design must meet at least some of the following:

1. *There needs to be a demonstrable representation of a multi-featured world with the organism within it.*
2. *The machine must show a sufficient understanding of its human interlocutors to be judged to be potentially conscious.*

3. *Reactive, contemplative and supervisory levels of reasoning must be discernable in the architecture that links perception to internal processing to action.*
4. *The machine could be characterized by low-level mechanisms that are equivalent to those known to be crucial to consciousness in the neurology of living mechanisms.*
5. *The machine must have means of demonstrably depicting and using the out-thereness of the perceived world and be able to use such depictions to imagine worlds and the effect of its actions.*
6. *Having adhered to some of the criteria above, the design must qualify what is meant by an emotional evaluation of the content of consciousness.*

– Aleksander, p88

Aleksander also points out that there are machines that we would not consider as conscious that do meet some of the above criteria. For example, the second criterion could be interpreted in such a way as to include a group of early AI programs that attempted to meet what is known as the Turing test. In this test laid out by Alan Turing in his 1950 paper Computing Machinery and

Intelligence he proposed to answer the question "Can machines think?" Simply put, the Turing test uses the complex nature of human dialogue as a test for human intelligence. In modern terms, we can imagine being engaged in an online chat using an instant messenger service and trying to determine whether we were chatting with a human or a machine. It turns out that it is possible to create a program that does a "good enough" job at mimicking human conversation, especially if the conversation is fairly mundane. Aleksander's point is that just meeting one of his criteria doesn't necessarily make a machine conscious. As a matter of fact he never really intends to build a rigid set of criteria for entrance into the consciousness club. His list is more of a list of what counts as progress toward that end. So exactly what does separate man from machines?

    One of the classic arguments against the possibility that machines can ever be conscious is known as the Chinese room. It was originally put forth by John Searle in his book <u>Minds, Brains, and Science</u> in answer to the question "can computers think?" This thought experiment is intended to demonstrate that computers are not in principle capable of thought. He considers a computer program which simulates the understanding of the Chinese language, that is, the computer can accept questions in Chinese and give appropriate answers, and compares this to putting a person into a locked room and having them accept Chinese characters and pass appropriate Chinese characters back out. The subject does not speak Chinese but has become adept at using a rule book which tells you how to respond when given a particular set of characters. This allows the person in the room to appear as if he is able to converse in Chinese when in fact he has no idea what he is saying. In Searle's words, "…from the point of view of an outside observer, you behave exactly as if you understood Chinese, but all the same you don't understand a word of Chinese." (Searle p33) What does this mean for our present investigation into the use of 'meaning', 'content', and 'semantics'? And what is the connection between these terms and the concept of 'understanding'? For Searle, "Understanding a language, or indeed, having mental states at all, involves more than just having a bunch of formal symbols. It involves having an interpretation, or a meaning attached to those symbols." (p33) In order to make this clearer, Searle contrasts this with asking and answering questions in English. Given the same situation, closed off in a room, you are passed questions in English that you are able to answer, such as 'What is your age?' The difference in this example according to Searle is that "you understand the questions in English because they are expressed in symbols whose meanings are known to you. ... In the case of the Chinese... you attach no meaning to any of the elements." (p34)

    Searle concludes that no machine can think by virtue of running a program because it has only syntax, no semantics. His view is that the computer program is a syntactic manipulation of symbols, but the symbols have no meaning, they are not about anything, they have no semantic content. Searle's definition of mind claims "...the mind has more than a syntax, it has a semantics. There is more to having a mind than having formal or syntactic processes. Our internal mental states, by definition, have certain sorts of contents." And lastly, "Minds are semantical, in the sense that they have more than a formal structure, they have a content." (p31)

    While Searle's analogy is a persuasive one, there is no evidence that the information in our brain, whether symbols or nerve impulses, carries an intrinsic semantic content any more than the symbols of the computer. He is unable to provide any argument that content exists besides what is carried by the symbols and their arrangement. What sense can we make of a distinction between the syntax and semantics of nerve impulses? I believe one of two possibilities to be the case. Either the distinction is an artificial one in which case there is no reason to pursue it, or we have defined and understood the problem so poorly that we will have to wait for a newer and better theory of consciousness so that we can reframe the problem in terms that will allow us to address it properly. In either case, I see no way to make further progress pursuing this line of thinking.

It's All Connected

One of the leading contenders in the attempt to provide intelligent machines is the *connectionist* approach. Believing that the limitation to simple meaningless symbols truly is a restriction on the level of intelligence attainable by machines, a group of people set out to create a new approach based loosely on the intricate interactions of the human brain. This model of mental processes has its roots in work on a model of computation known as the perceptron, an early and limited version of what has grown to become known as neural networks. One of its key proponents, Paul Smolensky has written extensively on this approach and addressed most of the arguments against it.

Smolensky claims that the distributed connectionist architecture is fundamentally different from the classical one. The key to this difference is that "mental representations and mental processes are not supported by the same formal entities – there are no 'symbols' that can do both jobs" (Smolensky p167). Smolensky believes the connectionist architecture provides the bridge between syntax and semantics. The connectionist architecture is split over two levels. According to Smolensky, the distributed connectionist models have the following two properties:

1. Interpretation can be assigned to large-scale activity patterns but not individual units.

2. The dynamics governing the interaction of individual units is sufficiently complex that the algorithm defining the interactions of individual units cannot be translated into a tractably specified algorithm for the interaction of whole patterns (p168).

The result of this characterization is that "the syntax ... resides strictly at the lower level while the semantics strictly resides at the upper level" (p168). This leads to the conclusion that an account cannot be provided in which the same elements of the model provide both the syntax and the semantics. It is for this reason that Smolensky claims that the distributed connectionist architecture is distinct from the classical one and not simply an implementation of it.

"Thoughts have composite structure" and "Mental processes are sensitive to this composite structure" (p169). Smolensky states "The resulting connectionist model of mental processing is characterized by context-sensitive constituents, approximately (but not exactly) compositional semantics, massively parallel structure-sensitive processing, statistical inference and statistical learning with structured representations" (p192).

Smolensky's account provides for an explanation of how a mind can have semantic content and yet still be tied to formally specified symbols with syntactically specified interactions. It should be acknowledged that this formal syntactic structure is not the symbol manipulation in the classical sense, although it is within the definition of a Turing machine, which is to say that anything that can be done in the connectionist model could be implemented by a Turing machine. While we have shown that it is possible to separate processes, computations, etc. into two or more layers, if we accept that the limits of the

Turing machine are what confine us to less than human intelligence, the connectionist model brings us no closer to our goal.

Discussion Points

Methodology and Scientific Explanation

One of the areas that lacks consensus in cognitive science is a methodology for testing for consciousness. It is one of the things that make it difficult for objective comparisons of findings in the research. Without a scientific community which uses a shared vocabulary to express their shared beliefs, it is difficult if not impossible to compare and discuss competing data and theories (Kuhn1970). I propose that to the extent that we believe modern psychology is on the right track (which I do), we should make use of its theoretical and clinical constructs as a starting point. In fact this is already done, but more among scientists than among philosophers. It might seem that we have little history on which to build when it comes to consciousness and even less when it comes to testing for consciousness in machines. But there is a similar model on which we can build – that of animal testing. Here as with machines, we test animals to better understand our own consciousness under the assumption that we can control the environment and the stimuli and draw parallels between the results with the animals and the state of human consciousness. This methodology has shown significant success and has gained wide acceptance in demonstrating the mental state of other beings (e.g. mice) where we cannot rely on communication as we would with other humans. For example, the efficacy of antidepressants in animal models of depression is based on predictive, face, and construct validity (Lucki).

Predictive validity is assessed by how well the effects of manipulations in the pathological state are mirrored in the animal model and is determined by the response of the model to antidepressant drugs. Research experiments attempt to demonstrate a positive response to known antidepressants and should not respond to ineffective agents. The goal is to show 'true positives' and 'true negatives' but not 'false positives'.

Face validity expresses the similarity between the animal model and the clinical disorder being examined in terms of symptoms and signs. In animal models of depression, this is the 'fit' of the clinical symptoms of the disorder and the changes in those symptoms in response to conventional treatment.

Construct validity is the correlation of the theoretical account of the model with the theoretical account of the disorder. There is a certain appeal to placing an exaggerated emphasis on construct validity over predictive and face validity. It must be remembered that the limits of our current understanding of pathologies such as depression force us to assess construct validity by evaluating whether behavior phenomena are correctly described.

Using the above as a model, a similar assessment of machine consciousness can be proposed. A non-prescriptive example for models of machine consciousness might include:

1. An MMC should be able to demonstrate a predictable set of behaviors in the domain of study according to an array of stimulus-response trials with some degree of certainty.
2. An MMC being tested according to the trials in (1) should be in a definable *state* similar to some hypothetical psychological state, e.g. aggressive/survival mode, nurturing mode.
3. There should be a theoretical account that explains why the predicted behavior should be expected under the

circumstances in (2) given the set of stimuli in (1).

The above is a very general description of validity that provides a framework without many details. By itself it is meaningless without specific trials in an attempt to demonstrate the application of specific theories of consciousness. Nonetheless, it provides three specific areas which I feel need to be addressed in any meaningful purported explanation of machine consciousness.

Managing Complexity - Consciousness Evolves

Understanding the connections between the neuronal activity in the brain and what we understand as consciousness is a daunting challenge. Many people have made an attempt to bring the concepts down to a manageable level by creating hypothetical universes occupied by hypothetical organisms. Dennett cites examples of these so-called "Democritean" universes (named by W.V.O. Quine for Democritus) and develops one such example of a two dimensional universe known as Conway's Life to reveal the concept of consciousness by viewing it from the evolutionary point of view. In this example of a universe there is a very simple set of laws by which we can predict very easily the state of any "atom" based solely on the eight atoms surrounding it. (Dennett refers to these atoms as pixels as this is implemented on a computer). This simple set of laws makes it relatively easy to work through scenarios and create collections of atoms in what resemble entities. These entities, or configurations as Dennett calls them, exhibit a simple yet predictable behavior. He notes that this creation of a behavior is done, and observed, at what he calls the *design level*, whereas the actual laws governing the state change from one time quantum to another are at the *physical level*.

When Dennett speaks of reasons for a particular action, or choice of action, he distinguishes between the reasons of the designer and the reasons of the agent itself. In the simpler designs, behavior is rather easily included through a "repertoire of reaction-tricks" (Dennett2003 p46) referring to what he calls *situation-action* machines. I assume Dennett would include such devices as the cruise control in a car in this category.

Dennett differentiates the *design stance* from the *intentional stance* in which we speak of entities as if they "know" or "believe" something, and "want to accomplish some end" (Dennett p45). As the agents and their behavior become more complex, the origin of the design is not clear. "If we ask "at what point" the designer's reasons become the designed agent's reasons, we may find that there is a seamless blend of intermediate steps, with more and more of the design work off-loaded from designer to designed agent." (Dennett2003 p46)

Dennett attempts to support this notion of *intentional stance* by pointing out that we tend to speak in a manner which assumes intentionality. "Our simplest doers have been reconceptualized as *rational agents* or *intentional systems* . . . We just assume that however they do it, they do it rationally – they draw the right conclusions about what to do next from the information they have, given what they want." (Dennett 2003 p.45) Dennett regards this intuition as supporting his theory of intentionality by saying this is just the way we speak; there is no reason to assume it has any bearing on the actual state of affairs. It sounds as thought Dennett regards this lack of distinction between humans and animals as evidence that there is no distinction to be drawn. But this distinction, as well as other sentient and non-sentient objects, could also be viewed as a less sophisticated taxonomy which has not yet been developed by an immature mind into "the true state of the universe" as described by Steve Mithen.

Of Mithen Men

Mithen follows in the footsteps of Merlin Donald, author of *The Origins of the Modern Mind*, in what he describes as 'cognitive archaeology'. While we already know that the brain has evolved over the millennia, Mithen assumes that the mind also evolved. It did this as a means of survival, with emphasis on skills that would aid in hunting and gathering. His perspective is evolutionary, trying to understand the nature of the human mind based on how it has changed and adapted over the millennia. These changes are not only physiological, but cultural developments. This is a significant distinction because while the cumulative developments of biological evolution are passed immediately upon birth (ignoring some developmental delays), the accumulated cultural progression is passed on only if and when the next generation is exposed to the learned behavior of its culture by surrounding adults.

To the case in point Mithen states: "This propensity to think of the natural world in social terms is perhaps most evident in the ubiquitous use of anthropomorphic thinking – attributing animals with humanlike minds. . . . The polar bear is thought of as a human ancestor, a kinsman, a feared and respected adversary. In the mythology of the Inuit there was a time when humans and polar bears could easily change from one kind to another." (Mithen1996 p48)

    In general, primitive cultures past and present think of their natural world as if it were a social entity. They fail to draw a distinction between the two. This trait is learned both by the culture and the individual. Even in the most advanced of cultures this is a trait that must be developed in the individual as witnessed by examples such as children talking to and interacting with toys. This lack of distinction is not limited to animals (live or stuffed) but includes typically inanimate objects as well (trains, blocks, and the like). Children in their early years act as though these objects share the same personal traits that they have come to expect from other people. So this type of behavior should not be viewed as 'the way the mind is' so much as a developmental phase in which more sophisticated skills, those of discrimination, have not yet been developed. As the individual or the culture develops, the ability to view entities as more varied and with different levels of sentience is acquired. It seems unlikely that an individual would develop this ability without the foundation of the culture, i.e. the social structure which supports our interpretation of our environment, but not necessarily impossible.

Limitations on Current Computers

There are many interesting areas worthy of investigation in the search for "more intelligent" computers. Much of what has been written about the limitations of machines is based on a set of problems that includes well-known and oft-quoted problems such as the halting problem, decidability, and incompleteness. While this is only a small subset of the problems that need to be addressed it is probably the most frequently raised objection to the possibility of "thinking machines." I will take a moment to try to put these problems into their proper perspective and show that the only limit they impose on machines is which design implementations will not yield the same level of thought we see in humans.

Kurt Gödel showed that in any formal system of arithmetic, if the system has a decidable set of formulas and if there is an effective method for telling whether or not something is a proof then that system is incomplete (Enderton p236). What this means in plain English is that any consistent formal system (mathematics, logic, etc.) there will be statements that are true that cannot be proven by a system of axioms and rules. In short, a formal system cannot be both consistent and complete. The *incompleteness* of these systems is what limits the power of the machines which implement them, namely computers of the current era.

It is not necessary to go into any more detail or to cite further examples as the point I want to make deals with a fundamental flaw in the argument typically made against the possibility that machines can think or otherwise be conscious. The simplified form of the argument is something like this (Searle p35):

1. Formal systems have known limitations on their expressiveness and power.
2. Computers use formal systems to control their actions.

Therefore – Computers are incapable of escaping their "formal" bounds and are precluded from "real" or meaningful thought.

Corollary – Humans are capable of thought and therefore must not think [exclusively] within the confines of a formal system.

The missing piece of this argument is that these limitations occur within a *single formal system*. This argument assumes that a computer is implemented within a single system of logic. Likewise, there is no consideration as to whether the same is true of human minds. Recent theories of mind make widespread use of hypotheses in which different parts of the brain function differently and are specialized to suit different types of tasks. Research in some of the more recent descendents of artificial intelligence relies extensively on modularization of tasks and specialized modules. It does not require any understanding of computer science or software engineering to see that it would be advantageous to be able to "shift gears" as befits the situation when attempting to solve complex problems. For example, there are statements that cannot be expressed in first-order logic (FOL) which can be expressed in higher order logics (HOL). For example, a simple statement such as "a set is finite" or "a set is countable" (has at most the same cardinality as the natural numbers), cannot be expressed in FOL. This is possible because second-order logic allows statements to include variables that range over sets of individuals whereas FOL restricts variables to individuals. It might seem that since HOLs are extensions of

FOL perhaps statements in HOLs are reducible to FOL statements but this is provably false as is the converse. Whenever we extend a logical system in one way, we sacrifice something else either in terms of expressive power, i.e. what we can say, or in terms of what we can prove. There are several important theorems of FOL that do not hold in second-order logic and in general second-order logic does not include a complete proof theory. There are many other variants of logic in which limitations of FOL are exceeded at the cost of some other property. There are logics which study only finite sets, logics in which variables range over subsets of the domain, and modal logics which address the notion of possibility.

With this added perspective the conclusion of the above argument deteriorates into:

Computers implemented with a single form of logic to implement their algorithms will be limited in their expressiveness and problem solving ability.

This perspective reduces the problem to an engineering challenge rather than granting it the metaphysical status afforded it by some. It is true there is no one system of logic in which we can represent and solve all of the problems that a human is capable of solving. It may even be true that there is no way to represent and solve these same problems in any combination of formal systems. But there is no reason to believe that formal systems are the only way to implement thinking machines. Isn't it possible that we may find it useful to implement some types of problems by having a machine throw a dart into a dart board? While this colorful example may not be a very practical way to implement a decision process, it illustrates the fact that formal mathematical systems are not the only way things get done in the world. Why would we want to start out designing an intelligent computer by restricting our options to them? There are many more interesting and promising areas to look at. The most promising at the moment is distributed computing.

Distributed Computing and Distributed Consciousness

Over the past decade we have seen an incredible growth in the World Wide Web. The Web is only one example of a trend in distributing computing resources. The concept of distributing computing resources is to take the various components and/or functions that for the first fifty years of computing were collocated in one box or at least one geographical location and spreading them across multiple locations. There are many designs, different ways of creating combinations, but the general concepts are the same. In many ways distributed computing is not new but only the next step in computer science principles that have been in existence and evolving for decades. For example, basic principles that gave rise to some of the first programming principles such as modularity, i.e., reuse of code, encapsulation of information, and minimizing the interdependency of modules is demonstrated by distributed computing. An oversimplified description of better living through distributed computing:

1) Increase computing power by using multiple resources, e.g. multiple processors rather than one;
2) Make computing more flexible, manageable, and ultimately more powerful by having information processing more modular and therefore specialized, e.g. we might have a resource that does nothing but analyze streams of text in search of interesting facts about genetics. This allows our "genetic analysis service" to be used and reused by many other services. It is a sort of "don't reinvent the wheel approach" which presumably allows us to refine this service more so than if we had

to develop and maintain a similar service every time we or anyone else has a need to perform the same task.

This second feature is what I believe will buy us meaningful advances in the IQ of computing machinery. Speed and power are certainly useful, but thinking back to the argument against thinking machines based on the limitations of formal systems, this is where the real fun begins.

As this trend develops, we will find that many of the more challenging tasks will be carried out in a distributed environment such as the web. Up until now, there hasn't been much discussion about the criterion for consciousness to be located in one place. Somehow it seems counterintuitive to speak of a conscious, sentient being existing in more than one place at the same time. There seems to be a presupposition that any living being has some specific location and it is singular. But is there any rational reason to make this assumption? Clearly, our brains are not located at one point, they are in some sense "spread out" and in fact we know they are at least in some sense distributed across many locations within our skulls. So what is the criterion for establishing a single unit of consciousness? Is there some maximum distance that can lie between all of the parts? Do they need to be contiguous?

Does Determinism Rule out Free Will?

Dennett claims that the traditional linking of determinism with inevitability is incorrect, as is indeterminism with "evitability" (Dennett2003 p56). Using the example of the Life world he points out that these pixel "organisms" are completely determined, i.e., you can run the same scenario as many times as you like and they will always result in the same outcome. Yet certain "organisms" will clearly be very good at avoiding threats. In our everyday way of thinking we might think this is not what we mean by an event or action being evitable, yet Dennett insists it is precisely the same thing.

These consistent outcomes raise a question for some. In systems such as a calculator, or even a very sophisticated computer, we expect consistent results. But we don't expect that in our own daily life we make the same decisions all of the time; we know that we don't always decide the same way. Dennett believes we should demand the same consistency in a conscious, sentient, decision-making being. But how do we obtain the flexibility without giving up the determination? We could always add an indeterministic element to allow this flexibility, but if free choices are *undetermined*, a Frankfurt type controller cannot control the subject's choices without intervening and forcing the agent to choose as he wants (Kane p88). While this may look like an impasse, there is one very key difference between our life and the Conway's synthetic life. Our life has many more variables in the inputs. Our world is vastly more complex. As Dennett points out, "they can get plenty of variability in the output of their faculties of practical reason by simply feeding in more varied input about their current state and circumstances" (Dennett2003 p111).

Dennett on Wegner, Wegner on Libet

For Dennett, the question "Does free will exist?" does not have a simple yes or no answer. The problem lies not in determining whether or not there really is something which exists that is responsible for making our decisions, i.e. something which belongs to each individual that can be said to make that individual responsible for their own actions, but rather it is with the entire notion of what we mean when we make such claims. Wegner downplays the role of consciousness in decision making:

> "Consciousness and action seem to play a cat-and-mouse game over time.
> …consciousness pops in and out of the picture and doesn't really do anything." (Wegner2002 p59)

Yet Dennett states very clearly that both he and Wegner believe that "responsible, moral action is quite real." (Dennett2003 p224) What Dennett is campaigning for is a more up to date understanding of what this free will is; in fact he claims that free will is not an illusion, as Wegner claims, but that we need to give up our outdated ideologies regarding free will. [The illusion is the need for a spiritual facet of free will] In the end, Dennett believes that the difference between Wegner and himself is mostly a matter of "expository tactic", but that both their accounts are naturalistic while leaving room for moral responsibility.

One of the problems that neuroscience raises is the notion of the "moral void". This term is a reference to a novel entitled *Brain Storm* by Richard Dooling in which one of the characters makes several references to Dennett's *Consciousness Explained*. Dennett points out that this character is an excellent example of how easily a typical person can understand everything Dennett has put forth in his theory of consciousness and yet incorrectly come to the conclusion that free will does not exist. The term "moral void" is a reference to the fact that there is a time of approximately 300 milliseconds in which the brain has begun processing stimuli, sensations, etc. before a person becomes aware of it. Since the processing which makes triggers a decision is preconscious, it would seem to some that there can be no sense in which a person can be morally responsible for that decision.

"When we remove the Cartesian bottleneck, and with it the commitment to the ideal of the mythic time t, the instant when the conscious decision happens, Libet's discovery of a 100-millisecond veto window evaporates. . . . Once you distribute the work done by the homunculus . . . you have to distribute the moral agency around as well. You are not out of the loop; you *are* the loop. . . . What you do and what you are incorporates all these things that happen and is not something separate from them." (Dennett2003 p241) It would seem that to say the consciousness does nothing is really just another category mistake. Wegner insists that conscious awareness of these activities is prerequisite to the notion of conscious agency. "The greatest contradictions to our ideal of conscious agency occur when we find ourselves behaving with no conscious thought of what we are doing" (Wegner2002 p157). It is clear that there are many activities taking place when we make a decision, and admittedly not all of them are subject to our review in the conscious stream. And although we may not yet be clear just how the conscious self participates in all decisions, we see evidence of a conscious aspect in many of these decisions – the veto scenario, the constant feedback scenario, and even the censor scenario are easily comprehended examples of situations where it is difficult to deny that there is some actively conscious intervention in our decision making.

Unconscious Actions – The Role of Ideomotor Actions

Many of our actions are initiated without our conscious intention. Wegner refers to this unconscious causation as the "fly in the ideal agent's ointment…" Wegner claims that by definition you are "out of the loop" of unconscious actions. As he points out, "you can't be conscious of everything you are doing – even holding perfectly still can be a variety of acts, not all of which you understand. ... This ghost army of unconscious actions provides a serious challenge to the notion of an ideal human agent. The greatest contradictions to our ideal conscious agency occur when we find ourselves behaving with no conscious thought of what we are doing" (Wegner2002 p157). But this type of behavior is not only common but necessary. I agree with Wegner that you can't be conscious of every detail of your actions; the conscious mind simply cannot manage that amount of information and decision making. We would slow almost to a halt if we had to consider every movement and decision as we drove down the busy streets of a city. Even typing these words requires hundreds of movements a minute in addition to considering what words to use. When learning any complex task it eventually becomes "second nature" out of necessity. The mind seems to automate tasks which do not need to be reevaluated each time they are performed while at the same time allowing for intervention by the conscious mind as necessary.

Even in making decisions we often utilize a sort of "short-circuit evaluation". Roger Schank has studied and developed this mental heuristic of storytelling or scripting. Consider some of the questions you are asked throughout the day. You walk into a restaurant and are asked, "Do you prefer smoking or non-smoking?" Most of us do not take the time to consider what this question entails even though there is always the outside possibility that during dinner we might decide to either quit or take up smoking – however remote that possibility might be. Why? Because we have answered this question many times before and there is little reason to believe our answer will or should be any different today and any possibility that we will change over dinner is so remote that the consideration does not warrant using up the limited resource of our conscious attention. So instead, we read from a rehearsed script. But this is not an abdication of our decision making authority; it is simply a delegation to some module of our mind which is ultimately under our command and control. Schank's theories are supported by recent evidence on decision making and the prefrontal cortex of the brain.

Higher level decision making is believed to reside primarily in the prefrontal cortex (PFC). More recently a role for the ventromedial prefrontal cortex (VMF) has been demonstrated through clinical studies of subjects with damage to the VMF. The findings are consistent with a second independently conducted fMRI study. These studies have established that the VMF is critical in decisions similar to real-life decisions, i.e., decisions involving outcomes which are uncertain in terms of either risk or ambiguity. The results suggest that the VMF is only involved in decisions that require actual assessment of the available choices. Where there is already a history of similar options and decisions it seems that patients are just as successful at making a choice from their autobiographical history of preferences. "The latter, possibly more commonly employed route would require recalling the fact that a particular option is a favorite, rather than relying on an ongoing, dynamic assessment of relative value." (Fellows2007 p5)

Dennett of course takes an evolutionary perspective on the dichotomy between ideomotor actions and conscious actions. "In most of the species that ever lived, "mental" causation has no need for, and hence does not evolve, any elaborate capacity for self-monitoring." (Dennett2003 p246) This seems plausible enough. Without the need for contemplating ethical dilemmas or devising intricate machinery or even board games for that matter, it seems most behavior in the animal kingdom could be explained, predicted, and implemented using a completely, well – behavioral system! "A bundle of situation-action links of indefinite sophistication can reside in the nervous system of a simple creature and serve its many needs without any further supervision" (Dennett2003 p247). From this Dennett draws the conclusion that there is no need in all but the most sophisticated animals (warm-blooded ones for example) for decisions to be monitored by anything or anybody. It seems plausible that in the very near future we could create animal robots that mimic a given animal to within the criteria of a Turing test. So it would seem that up to the point of what we call in rather loose terms "animal behavior" or "animal consciousness" we could replicate using implementation methods not very different than what is technologically feasible today. I would grant that there are levels of consciousness such as those seen in most animals that do not require an elaborate mechanism for self-monitoring, but Dennett has only shown this to be the case as long as we exclude the type of consciousness we see in humans. When we turn our attention to these higher functions, we see a distinct need for some additional mode of thought processing.

Volition

We are able to detect the difference between voluntary and involuntary actions. We are all familiar with the fake smile. It doesn't look the same as a real smile. In some cases, we can measure differences neurologically between voluntary and involuntary actions. But the line is not always clear between the two and in fact often our voluntary actions become involuntary over time the more we practice tem. Anyone who has any experience with any sport from golf to kickboxing knows that the secret to becoming proficient is to practice until you no longer have to think about what you are doing. It may seem that this automation of tasks disproves the need for a theory of volition within the theory of mind. But if we view this as a transition from a learning mode to what we might call "high performance" mode, it is all just part of the adaptation process. But then where does volition fit into this hypothesis? I don't believe that we currently know enough about the details of the learning and adaptation process to answer this question, but we can present a plausible hypothesis which will at lest demonstrate that the existence of volition is not precluded by the automation scenario. (Note that it is also inconsequential whether or not the system in which volition itself resides is located in one place in the brain or is a network of neurons throughout the brain.)

    To begin with, let's make a couple of assumptions that seem to be workable with regard to where these actions originate in the brain. Let's say that actions of a deliberative nature take place in the pre-frontal cortex (PFC) and that actions of an automatic nature take place in some module of the appropriate type. I am using the term *module* to refer to some functionally specialized section of the brain, without any concern for where the module actually resides or even whether it is located in one location or distributed over many areas of the brain.

It seems plausible that the center of volition could participate in the deliberation taking place in the PFC. This story maps easily to the scenario where we sit and contemplate whether or not to get up and walk across the room.

Baars cites a study by Langer and Imber in which they attempt to show that conscious access to an action is a necessary condition of avoiding incorrect execution of tasks which have become automatic. Results of the study show that if a task is presented which is expected to produce a high rate of error in the test subject, the more the task was practiced the easier it was to get the subject to produce errors. "These results suggest that three things go together: consciousness of action details, voluntary control over those details, and the ability to monitor and edit the details. Indeed, the ability to monitor and edit a planned act – to be *responsible* for it – may be the essence of voluntary control." (Baars1997 p136) There is a tradeoff between the efficiency of automaticity and the success of deliberate consideration.

Often, even our automatic actions are not entirely without conscious intervention. We might say to ourselves, "I can't hear the TV, I need to turn up the volume," and then without consciously thinking about the details, reach for the remote, find the appropriate button and turn up the TV. This is a simple example of how we can deliberately initiate actions which are mostly executed non-voluntarily. It also presents a justification for how even automatic actions are the result of our intentions and therefore are still subject to our responsibility. There will, of course, be situations in which we consider external influences, mitigating circumstances, which may absolve us of at least some responsibility, such as the case of the fire and the coffee pot. I consider these to be limiting factors on personal responsibility which do not impinge on the validity or plausibility of the theory.

Integration of the Conscious Mind and the Automatic Modules

Most of us are familiar with phenomena such as dowsing rods and Ouija boards. The key point of these types of demonstrations is that some object or objects, the indicator on the Ouija board or the dowsing rods, are made to move in some supposedly meaningful manner without the conscious intervention of the person wielding them. What makes these devices seem mystical to some is the ability to respond to "forces" that do not originate within us. What is actually happening of course is that our intentions, either conscious or subconscious, are influencing various automatic functions in out brain. Baars believes this demonstrates the validity of his theater architecture. "Conscious goals can activate many unconscious action plans and motor routines." (Baars1997 p138)

In many of our day to day activities it does seem that there is a very closely integrated balance of cooperation between the conscious and the automatic functions of the mind. One of the best and most common examples is the way we speak. As our speaking skills become more and more developed, we get better at putting together long, detailed, complex groups of sentences extremely quickly. All you have to do is watch someone speaking in a heated argument to realize that they couldn't possibly be deliberating over the choice of every word. But even when we are speaking very quickly, we are very good at catching and correcting our mistakes. We correct our pronunciations, grammatical mistakes, and even correct our sentences when we feel there is some subtle unintended meaning that we might have spoken more eloquently. All of this we do without having to understand the mechanics (or neuroscience) underlying this amazing accomplishment. Baars concludes that "… unconscious systems seem to be far more subtle and complex and seem to "make use of" conscious information in a distributed sense." (Baars1997 p139) This type of activity is a prime example of an instance in which our mind is more analogous to the efforts of a finely tuned team of specialists than it is to hierarchical modules. Although there are undoubtedly examples of simple mental activities in which processing passes quietly from one module to the next and on to the next, it seems likely that our more impressive cognitive abilities are processed with a constant and frequently changing flow of information back and forth between multiple modules, constantly monitoring, checking, correcting, refining, and sometimes deciding on ideas and actions.

Cause and Effect

The concept of *causation* is not easy to define in any way that covers our broad use of the term. As we try to describe the relationship between causation and necessity we often seem to run into contentious explanations. We use the term all the time both in everyday language as well as in scientific discourse, yet it is difficult to say what counts as causation except by example. When we say the baseball caused the window to break, we mean that if it had not been for the baseball's existence at that particular place and flying through the air at some speed, we would not have had the effect of the window breaking. We can be more specific by speaking of *causal necessity* vs. *causal sufficiency*.

Causal sufficiency states that given a particular condition (the cause) the resulting effect is inevitable. Whenever the baseball hits the window at some speed, the result is that the window breaks – this is the inevitable outcome.

Causal necessity states that a particular condition is necessary for a particular outcome to occur. Using our baseball example, this would mean that in all possible cases where the window breaks, it was caused by the baseball. At first glance it may seem that causal necessity and sufficiency are equivalent, two different ways of saying the same thing. To be more clear, for causal necessity to hold, it must be the case that had the baseball not been thrown, the window would not have broken. If this still sounds like the same thing it is because this is the way people talk. But in everyday speech, what people really mean is that had the baseball not been thrown there is a high probability that the window would not have broken. Our definition is more like saying that there is no way for the window to break without throwing the baseball at it. Another condition usually applied to the identification of causes is what Dennett refers to as *temporal priority*. This is the assumption that for an effect to be linked to a cause, the cause must precede the effect in time.

Possible Worlds and Other Jedi Mind-Tricks

In our deliberations we often consider how things could or could not have happened. We imagine *possible worlds* in which we try to carry out to their logical conclusion scenarios in which *we might have done otherwise*. These hypothetical case studies are used both in our own day to day life and in philosophical arguments such as the Luther example or Frankfurt-type examples.

In discussing the possible worlds scenarios Dennett describes a type of informal predicate called *identification predicates* of the form "is Socrates." This notion relies on the hypothesis that we consider someone in another world to be "the same person" as the one in this world if they share a certain collection of features. (Dennett2003 p66) In the actual world in which we live we believe that when we apply the "is Socrates" predicate to someone – This man is Socrates – we know how to verify the truth of this statement and we also know that it can apply to only one such person.

But when we begin to talk about applying this predicate to individuals in other worlds we become less certain about what it means to be Socrates. If we imagine a candidate who seems to be exactly like Socrates in every possible way at same place and time as we would expect Socrates to be except for the fact that he can fly like Superman, can we still apply the predicate "is Socrates" or have we wandered outside the boundaries of what it is to be Socrates? On the one hand, if we take the stand that a persons is who they are by virtue of their characteristics, then any discourse on hypothetical worlds in which that person is any different become nonsense. But if we want to allow discussions on possible worlds, how do we draw the line between different scenarios for the same person and different persons in the same scenario? This is an important distinction and is a matter of contingent properties versus essential or necessary properties (Leibniz p97). It allows us to distinguish between the point in our hypothetical situation where we have effectively replaced one person with a totally different person and the case where we have not.

In the search for a responsible self we have seen that far from being totally autonomous, we must concede that we are to some extent at the mercy of external factors. Even if we maintain that we make our own decisions, just by virtue of the limitations of the possible choices from which we have to choose we are under the partial control of others. But how are we to differentiate between the benign influence of our peers and mentors and the insidious manipulation of some evil neuroscientist deliberately brainwashing us to his own ends?

Consider a counterfeit dollar perfect to the last detail and only you know it is counterfeit – let's say you made it yourself so nobody but you knows. It is so perfect that it withstands the scrutiny of every expert in existence. We have proven exhaustively that this "must be a genuine dollar" and have left no test untried. Anyone would claim that this truly is a genuine dollar, why would they not? What exactly does this mean? You know it is counterfeit. The "authorities" know it is *genuine*. How do these two claims differ? There is absolutely no physical difference between the counterfeit dollar and any other genuine dollar. The *only* feature that differentiates them is their history. We say the counterfeit dollar does not have the proper origin or provenance. It doesn't meet our criteria for how it came to be in existence.

Dennett recounts a similar example where we have two subjects, Ann and Beth, identical twins who are psychologically identical. They both act alike, have the same personality, etc. Ann is truly autonomous (however that might be possible). Beth believes she is autonomous, but has been tricked into thinking this. The two are completely indistinguishable except by the knowledge of this fact. Like the counterfeit dollar, we might claim that they differ, but only by the fiat of provenance. (Dennett2003 p282) This seems like an artificial and unjustifiable distinction.

The above types of difficulty are common in philosophical discussions precisely because they are hypothetical. Philosophical discussions are not limited by what we can create in a laboratory. Some might say they are not limited by common sense. But such difficulties are not limited to the ramblings of philosophers. Einstein's thought experiments and even more recent work in theoretical physics (think string theory) are not conducted in the laboratory. Hypotheticals offer great flexibility by removing practical and even physical limitations, i.e., the known laws of physical science. If we like we can imagine worlds in which bodies are not limited by the speed of light or where we can move backwards in time. Perhaps these are just philosopher mind-tricks, engineered to convince the weak of something that simply could not be true. "You are responsible for your own actions!" "Free will is an illusion!"

    At an intuitive level, we all believe that we cause our own behavior. We don't necessarily know the inner mechanics of either our body or our mind, yet we presume that this series of causes and effects, the end result which we call our decisions and our behavior, is under the control of our will. Wegner compares our belief in the causal chain of our free will with the *perceived causal sequence* in a magician's illusion. There is a *real causal sequence* of events which explains the trick. Because we do not notice them, we interpret the result erroneously. Wegner claims we make the same error when we conclude that we control our own actions. While it is true that we control our own actions in the sense that our action is a result of a great many physical and mental processes, the notion that there is a *will* or some conscious *intention* that makes the decision is just an illusion. "We can't possibly know (let alone keep track of) the tremendous number of mechanical influences on our behavior because we inhabit an extraordinarily complicated machine. So we develop a shorthand, a belief in the causal efficacy of our conscious thoughts. We believe in the magic of our own causal agency" (Wegner2002 p27).

Dennett sees Wegner's analogy as a half-truth. He believes that Wegner is correct about the illusory nature of the will, but that he is wrong in the conclusions he draws from this. He notes that Wegner uses the imagery of a person inhabiting a machine, which according to Dennett puts him right back into the Cartesian Theater.

James, is it really necessary?

Let's take a step back for a moment to consider whether Wegner's causal sequence argument is a compelling as it at first may seem. While it is true that (1) when we don't have all of the facts we may draw incorrect conclusions, Wegner also hangs a lot of weight on the fact that (2) we develop a "shorthand" which leaves out many of the intervening details. These two facts are not at all connected. Consider an example from your favorite spy film. There are many so I will select one at random, a James Bond film. We witness some high tech device which will be used in an attempt to kill Mr. Bond, a laser perhaps. Having turned on the laser, the arch villain Goldfinger announces to our hero "No Mr. Bond, I expect you to die." Now you don't get to be an arch villain like Goldfinger without being very smart, undoubtedly a genius; so we can assume that Goldfinger probably does know the many inner workings of the laser and that his decision to kill Bond would be effected exactly as he intends. Most of us would concede that Goldfinger had caused Bond's death (if it weren't for Bond's incomparable wit allowing him to bluff his way out of the situation). But suppose Goldfinger had instead sent one of his bumbling henchmen to kill Bond. This uneducated lackey may not understand the difference between a laser and a flashlight – not in terms of physics anyway. He just knows that when you flip the switch on a laser, it hurts a lot more than a flashlight. So he understands the end result of turning on a laser when a living human being is in its path, and most courts would undoubtedly find him responsible for killing Mr. Bond or anyone else who fell victim to his laser. Can we imagine anyone arguing that because he couldn't possible understand or even be aware of all of the many electronic parts that are needed to produce this high quality beam of light, the fact that the defendant threw the switch really doesn't make him responsible for Mr. Bond's death. The point is, although Wegner and Dennett are correct to say that the more complex a series of events linked by cause and effect become the more chance there is that the casual observer (whether in a magic show or in the Cartesian theater) may draw erroneous conclusions. It does not, however, follow that for a person to be the "owner" of their actions, they need to know all of the mechanical or mental influences that are part of the causal sequence which brings about that action.

    Much of the literature focuses on where the critical junctures reside, within the conscious being or external to it. In fact, even at a vernacular level, we often find examples of the appellations "battle of the will" of "test of will power. There is no reason to believe that there is some single cause, or collection of causes, that lie either internal or external to the conscious entity. Rather, it is a completely viable explanation to assume that the agent and its environment coexist in a network of events, causes and effects if you like, an ecosystem in which at any given moment there are simultaneous (or nearly simultaneous) interactions, some of which occur across the boundaries of what we call the self.

In this view of the world, decisions by an agent are essentially the set of events related to the outcome in question which lie within the purvey of the agent in question. To some extent this may be viewed as an arbitrary delineation insofar as the psychodynamics of the decision is concerned.

The real issue is practical predictability or *practical control*. Take an example of a complex dynamic system such as the weather. Are the results consistent? Do we get the same results every time the same circumstances are presented? On an elementary level, yes. We can make predictions such as "Given certain atmospheric conditions related to wind, temperature, and pressure, precipitation will take the form of snow rather than rain." But if we push this predictability to a more granular level, the task becomes more difficult. How much snow will fall next year on March 1 between four and six o'clock? The reason for the difficulty as we extend our theories beyond simple *controlled* circumstances is that we find it more difficult to apply these completely deterministic laws in such a complex dynamic system. (By "extending our theories" we really mean extending the reach of our theories. The theories themselves aren't changed, only their application or articulation with the empirical world.)

Consider an analogous situation in psychology. Can we predict the behavior given a set of conditions? Of course! We do it all the time, even more often with laboratory mice. We might predict with all but absolute certainty that when we put a human subject in a controlled environment and apply a stimulus such as a drug, the subject will respond by exhibiting some behavior with probability X. But what happens when we try to extend our theories of psychology to make predictions such as "Next year on March 1 between four and six o'clock the subject will be thinking X and will decide A." We are at a loss, not because the tenets of psychology fail us, but chiefly because the large number of variables cannot be controlled and this uncertainty in our data makes it impossible in a practical sense to calculate the probability of the resulting behavior.

The apparent uncertainty in human behavior, human decisions, and therefore free will if primarily due to limitations in our ability to make predictions about events beyond a certain horizon with more than a few variables. This no more invalidates the bearing of the completely determined laws of a complete psychology (laws still not completely understood) than our inability to accurately predict the weather any further than several days invalidates the laws of physics.

Conclusion

The classical model of consciousness served its purpose and fit as an explanatory tool which seemed to match our observations for many centuries. But over the past century we have seen increasing difficulties in accounting for our observations as our knowledge of psychology and neuroscience uncovers more of the biology, chemistry, and even physics underlying the behavior and mental state of the human mind. This common view of consciousness has outlived its usefulness. Likewise, our simplistic and mystical view of free will is longer up to the task of serving a useful purpose in our network of beliefs. As both Wegner and Dennett would say, it is the end of free will as we know it. The illusion is not that we have free will, but that there is a separate and distinct *thing* that governs our mind.

A Brave New Paradigm

What will future research into theories of mind look like and in what directions should we search for the answers to the difficult questions? Thomas Kuhn has pointed out that as science progresses it reaches milestones in which major shifts in thinking are not just a result of progress but necessary for that progress. Distinct paradigm shifts including changes in views, concepts, language use, and entire theories are required to solve the problems at hand. "One aspect of every revolution is, then, that some of the similarity relations change. Objects which were grouped in the same set before are grouped in different sets afterwards and *vice versa*" (Kuhn1970 p204). While Kuhn has commented that his critics find his positions relativistic, there is at least one sense in which this progress through revolution can be measured objectively. "Later scientific theories are better than earlier ones for solving puzzles in the quite often different environments to which they are applied" (Kuhn1970 p206). A theory of consciousness should solve problems in the empirical world.

If we believe Kuhn's depiction of scientific progress, we have to admit that we cannot make significant progress until we can move into a paradigm suited to the theoretical models we need to construct to address the questions we face. How do we go about searching for such a paradigm? It's not as simple as coming to a fork in the road and taking the road less traveled. It is more like realizing that we are on the wrong continent and that the continent we need to be on hasn't been discovered yet. In fact, this type of paradigm discovery (we might say the only true sense of paradigm discovery) lies at the heart of what we typically call creative genius. Einstein is quoted as saying, "The significant problems we face cannot be solved at the same level of thinking we were at when we created them." But even the Einsteins of the world don't know how to make such revolutionary discoveries at will. Does this leave us at the mercy of fate, waiting for someone to have the answer revealed to them in a dream? We cannot provide a method for paradigm discovery, but we can direct our research in some useful way.

The clinical constructs mentioned above are one example of establishing validity of a hypothesis. This is as good a proto-example as any. It is not meant to be prescriptive but rather to be suggestive of what a realistic methodology might look like. Any theory of mind should be able to demonstrate that it offers at least a plausibly productive way to proceed. The study of consciousness and volition like all of cognitive science is a large and diverse field and the subject matter is complex so naturally the framework for scientific investigation and explanation should be expected to vary widely. What counts as an appropriate explanatory structure in deliberation might not make sense in the study of ideomotor function. The goal should be to have, in each area of the field, a generally accepted approach for theoretical explanation and validation. This will, however, require the emergence of a unified community within those fields and in cognitive science in general. In the meantime, we must accept that we will be saddled with the inefficiencies of competing paradigms.

One of the key misconceptions we have fallen into in the past is the notion that concepts such as free will and consciousness can be neatly categorized into discrete taxonomies. This is not just a question of granularity, not a question of not having enough categories. It is not just as simple as saying we cannot draw a simple distinction between conscious and non-conscious animals or between those possessing free will or not. Otherwise, the solution would be to better define consciousness or free will so we can better categorize which mammals are conscious and which are not. Or we might claim, "If you mean this type of consciousness we require qualities A, B, and C; if you mean this type of consciousness X and Y must also be present." But the nature of concepts such as these is that they are a continuous spectrum, as demonstrated in Dennett's examples of evolution. There are parts of the spectrum where we can clearly see that all of set X are intentional, or are conscious, or have free will. There are areas where the members in that neighborhood of the spectrum clearly are not intentional, or conscious, or do not have free will. But if we try to establish clear boundaries between the two, we can never establish a set of criteria by appealing to our scientific theories. These thresholds can only be set by fiat. Certainly such thresholds are necessary as operational guidelines, but it is a mistake to believe they exist as part of the laws of nature. We draw these lines in the sand as a necessary part of our existence. They are a necessary and useful part of our policies, our legal system, and our social apparatus. They cannot and should not be abolished, although the actual location of these demarcations will move over time. The distinctions will shift with changes in social norms and legal adjudication and these changes should be informed by our growing understanding of the science that seeks to explain them.

Revised Criteria for Human-like Consciousness

What kinds of criteria might we expect to establish for the consciousness of machines? One of the more obvious qualities, one often associated with higher levels of intelligence, is that of meta-thought. The ability to effectively think and communicate in meta-terms is a strong differentiator between humans and other life forms. Not only can we think and speak about an object in front of us but we can consider the situation in which we find ourselves with that object. We consider questions such as "Is it a threat?" We can imagine ourselves and the object in other situations and ask "How could I benefit from this object?" We can even think about our situation in some abstract language such as first-order logic or in a meta-language. These are all examples of the ability to think and communicate in true languages, not just the one word commands such as we use to train our dogs. We have the capacity for hierarchies of thought and second-order sentences – sentences about the sentences. It is very possible that a key differentiator between beings capable of moral agency and those which are not is the ability for well-developed communication.

A second differentiator is that humans seem to be constantly reviewing and adjusting their view of the world around them. We have seen that consciousness thought of the level we ascribe to humans needs to include some sort of feedback loop in the architecture of the part or parts of the system that provides what we have come to call higher consciousness. Decisions are often the result of deliberation and evaluation. Once patterns or scripts have been established, decision making can be delegated to functional units, semi-autonomous action-response machines, capable of making decisions. Machines worthy of being called conscious will need to be capable of reflection and deliberation. This will always require, at least for some scenarios, a supervisory role for some agent or module and a means by which the intervention of this module can be invoked under the appropriate circumstances.

Volition in Machines

To what end do we ask questions about volition and the moral agency of machines? Is the question whether a machine can be held legally responsible for its actions? Are we considering elevating some machines to the legal status of a competent individual? Or are we simply asking whether a machine can form intentions and to what extent we can trust machines with important decisions? We already trust machines to take the controls of an airliner with hundreds of people aboard; although not without supervision! When we consider the ability of machines to make decisions of their own free will, there is an insinuation that we are asking whether or not they have a mind. We have seen no evidence so far suggesting that the two need to be connected in this way. Despite our tendency to speak in terms that imply consciousness, I believe the criteria for free will and responsibility are distinct from those that are required for consciousness. That is not to say that there are no interactions between the two, perhaps even interdependencies, but we have seen nothing essential in either that makes one a necessary condition of the other. I think it is possible to establish a few useful guidelines for establishing volition in machines without sliding back into the false sense of certainty of developing an exhaustive set of criteria. But first I want to review the nature of responsibility and the problems that some see with the infinite regress in establishing responsibility from causes.

    We have seen that when we try to establish responsibility for a person's actions through an unbroken chain of causes we encounter one problem or another. It seems that this approach either leads to causes that precede our existence or that lie outside of us and outside of our control. Neither conclusion leaves us with the level of personal responsibility we expect of ourselves. We have again fallen into the trap of looking for a single point where we become responsible for our actions. The nature of responsibility is that it shifts from one place to another. It moves from one person to another or from several persons to several others. In some cases it shifts from a set of circumstances to a person. (In this example some might be bothered by suggesting that a set of circumstances has its own moral agency, for them it might make more sense to say that the responsibility develops in the person.) In all of these cases, the progressive assignment of responsibility results in a spectrum. When we speak of assignment of responsibility we often talk in terms that suggest responsibility falls into rather distinct categories. "The fault was all his." or "The fault lay mostly with the defendant." But these assessments are only snapshots of the circumstances resulting from a particular viewpoint. It would serve us better to say that responsibility accrues to the individual. This model better depicts the responsibility in specific situations. Just as importantly it represents our development over time. There is no point when a child becomes a responsible adult. There is no point when the causes of their actions become their own. This transformation by accrual occurs along with a change in the field of possible choices. Luther's statement of the possibility that he could do otherwise was as much a statement of what his possible choices had become as to how he had gotten to that point in his life.

    As a demonstration of this limitation of choices, consider a game of chess. Move by move Player 1 becomes more and more certain to win, Player 2 to lose. Each has the "free will" to choose their next move from all possible moves. Note that when we say *all possible moves* we mean all legal moves open at that point in the game given the situation on the board at that time. The range of moves is limited by the current circumstances and the rules of the game. As the game progresses, we can imagine thinking, of Player 1 perhaps, "the winner is already determined." Certainly we do not mean to imply that the winner was determined from the start. We only mean that as the game progresses, there are fewer and fewer choices that would allow Player 2 to win, until ultimately the chances wane to zero. Just as the range of moves in the chess game is limited by the current circumstances and the rules of the game, a person's choices are limited by, for example, their geographical location and the laws of physics.

Admittedly, our acts do not occur in a vacuum, without connections to our past decisions, influenced only by pure will. Our will, our self, like the chess game, is constantly and continually progressing, developing, evolving. Each act, each decision, and each resulting effect in some way determines the nature of the individual self, in some sense dictating that given a particular circumstance we "could do no other." To the extent that our responsible self develops within a culture, within a society, that responsibility develops along with it. In this way responsibility must be assigned by society and accepted by the self. The assumption of responsibility is a part of the decision making process. This is not to say that not accepting responsibility for one's moral agency precludes assignment of responsibility. But this mutual allocation of responsibility is part if the process in determining that responsibility.

There are a number of flaws in the way we perceive change. The notion of essentialism leads us to believe that if something "is Socrates" then there must be a definitive list of what it is to be Socrates. Likewise, we want to believe we can create a list of the features that define the criteria for consciousness. These categories are fictions, useful, possibly necessary fictions but fictions nonetheless.

There is also a flaw in the way we perceive causes and effects as discrete objects. Even the temporal aspect of cause and identity is suspect. For some years the field of physics has struggled with the unification of their theories as we discover more and more empirical evidence to challenge our views. While it is itself not a mature theory, string theory offers a challenge to our common sense perspective which may have implications for causal theory and therefore for theories of free will.

We have seen how characteristics such as intention can evolve in even simple organisms, both in the real world and in computer simulations. Even though there are no components of intention in the individual cells, the organism as a whole exhibits behavior which seems to demonstrate intent. We can define the intent of an agent as some collection of its demonstrated behavior. There is no evidence for any dualism between the cells of the organism and the "stuff of intent" yet the behavior is undeniable.

The sum total of what it means for an agent to be autonomous is put succinctly by Dennett: "The genuinely autonomous agent is rational, self-controlled, and not wildly misinformed"

(Dennett2003 p284). Based on the above conclusions, the following is a proposed set of criteria for responsible, free, conscious agents:

> *An agent is free, in a meaningful sense, if and only if it acts according decisions under its own control, i.e. it acts autonomously.*
>
> *An agent is responsible for its actions if and only if it acts according to its own intentions, i.e. it has acted without control by other autonomous agents.*
>
> *While not strictly necessary, a general awareness of an agent's environment and of the resulting effect of interacting with its environment demonstrates a higher degree of responsibility.*
>
> *Reactive, contemplative and supervisory levels are necessary to allow any meaningful level of reasoning or problem solving ability in a dynamic environment.*

The development of specialized organs in mammals and their cooperative nature within the system suggests how collections of specialized cells can be integrated into a modular system capable of functionality far beyond anything that could possibly achieved by an conglomerations of like cells. Extending this model to the distributed computing architecture it seems likely that machines fitting the above criteria will utilize some form of distributed processing, not necessarily under the control of a single physical unit. Currently, the most prominent example of such an environment is the World Wide Web. The web provides many of the prerequisites in terms of modularity and flexibility, and is a likely medium for at least the first wave of machines with human-like consciousness and autonomy. The exact nature of such a distributed intelligence or distributed consciousness is not clear. We may not even be aware that such intelligent, autonomous agents have emerged until after they have.

Levels of Evolution – The Starter Life

We have seen how the notion of evolution applies not only to the biological and genetic changes in organisms but to their behavior as well. The phenomenon of evolution is seen not only as the evolution of behavior patterns in single organisms, but is also observable in the behavior and behavior patterns that develop in a society or a group through cultural learning. Evolution is the emergence of new characteristics as viewed at the organism or species level as well as the social or cultural level. In addition to these two levels, a third level can be viewed through the lens of evolution.

Anyone who has seen Jurassic Park knows that at one time dinosaurs ruled the earth. But as the earth matured, the ecosystem evolved. Through some series of circumstances the planet itself evolved from a collection of cold-blooded lizard-brains to warm-blooded mammals capable of rapid learning and more importantly, cultural evolution. The earth cast aside the dinosaurs once they had served their purpose in developing its biosystem and ultimately replaced them with homo-sapiens. Of course, this process was far more than a two step process. There were many steps in between, and many steps that preceded the Jurassics.

Closing Comment

Rise of the Machines

As the biosystem that is the earth develops at a design level and an intentional level, will homo-sapiens develop as well? Or will a different species emerge? Having moved from unicellular to multicellular, from cold-blooded to warm-blooded, from invertebrate to vertebrate, will the next step be a further biological and genetic enhancement? Or is it possible that we are approaching the limits of the carbon-based biological sentient life form? Will mother earth give birth to a race of conscious machines to move the planet to the next level? Perhaps this strays into the realm of science fiction, but it is just as believable that the role of homo-sapiens is to be the medium for the development of the technological and cultural basis for machines without the same limits of mammals.

The Next Chapter

What exactly does it mean to say a person it intelligent? We often hear someone say, "He's really intelligent". We even hear people say, "Dolphins are intelligent". But what exactly does it mean to say someone is intelligent? Are we merely suggesting that they have the ability to answer questions correctly; or perhaps to solve difficult problems? Or do we mean they have the ability to communicate? As far as we know humans are the only creatures that communicate using what we commonly refer to as language, despite the fact that many animals are able to communicate to some extent without a language.

This book has focused primarily on the notion of free will in non-organic mechanisms. But the notion of intelligence is perhaps more interesting, more easily addressed, and probably a more imminent issue. We already know machines (typically the genre referred to as computers) are very good at certain tasks: mathematical calculations, processing large amounts of data, making certain types of decisions quickly and consistently. Give a computer a well-defined rule for when to buy 1000 shares of a particular stock and will execute flawlessly. Given a well-written program, we have seen that a car can drive down the street without a human driver. Some cars now have systems that supersede the judgment of their human driver, applying the brakes when the human operator fails to perform in time. Indeed, there is a certain set of problems that the silicon beast excels far beyond what any human can do. Yet, most of us would not admit that any of these silicon units possess true intelligence. Is there truly some criterion which they fail to meet, or is this simply the newest manifestation of bigotry?

Many scientists, philosophers, and countless others have conjectured about the reasons that a computer cannot ever possess the same sentient qualities of a human. They range from claims that a computer does not have a soul to the assumption that a computer is not capable of reflection or self-awareness. Sometimes it is as simple as "Can a computer really think?" or "Can a machine consider its relevance to the rest of the world."

When I sat down to write an addition to the second edition of this book I wanted to expand on this notion of intelligence but I quickly realized that our progress in technology has already moved beyond the imagination of most science fiction writers. The various aspects that need to be addressed are many and the implications are probably beyond our comprehension. For this reason, I decided to begin working on an entirely new set of essays to consider the questions of intelligence, computing mechanisms, and the other questions that will inevitably emerge. As I began contemplating my list of questions which I feel should be addressed, I formulated an initial working thesis of sorts:

How Computers Can Do Everything We Can Do – Only Better

And so I conclude what I first thought would be the next and final chapter to this second edition with no new answers…no new conclusions, and not so much as a well thought out list of questions.

June 5, 2014

References

Aleksander, Igor, 2007. "Machine Consciousness", The Blackwell Companion to Consciousness. Blackwell Publishing Ltd.

Austen J.L., 1962. How to do Things with Words, Harvard University Press.

Baars, Bernard J, 1997. In the Theater of Consciousness: The Workspace of the Mind, Oxford University Press.

Chalmers, David, 2007. "The Hard Problem of Consciousness", The Blackwell Companion to Consciousness, Wiley-Blackwell.

Dennett, Daniel, 2003. Freedom Evolves, Penguin Books.

Enderton, Herbert B, 2001. A Mathematical Introduction to Logic, Harcourt Academic Press.

Fellows, Lesley K., Farah, Martha J., 2007. "The Role of Ventromedial Prefrontal Cortex in Decision Making: Judgment under Uncertainty or Judgment Per Se?", Cerebral Cortex. Oxford University Press.

Frankfurt, Harry G, 1988. "Alternate Possibilities and Moral Responsibility", The Importance of

What We Care About: Philosophical Essays, Cambridge University Press.

Ginet, Carl, 1962. "Can the Will be Caused?", The Philosophical Review, Vol. 71, No. 1, (Jan., 1962), pp. 49-55, Duke University Press.

Ginet, Carl, 1996. "In Defense of the Principle of Alternative Possibilities: Why I Don't Find Frankfurt's Argument Convincing", Nous, Vol 30, Philosophical Perspectives, 10, Metaphysics, Blackwell Publishing.

Hall, James W., 1978. "Deciding as a Way of Intending", The Journal of Philosophy, Vol. 75, No. 10 (Oct., 1978), pp. 553-564.

Hempel, Carl G., 1965. Aspects of Scientific Explanation. The Free Press.

Hobbes, Thomas, 1962. Leviathan. Touchstone Edition, Simon & Schuster.

Kane, Robert, 2005. A Contemporary Introduction to Free Will. Oxford University Press.

Kuhn, Thomas, 1970. "Reflections on my Critics", Criticism and the Growth of Knowledge, Cambridge University Press.

Libet, Benjamin, 2004. Mind Time: The Temporal Factor in Consciousness (Perspectives in Cognitive Neuroscience), Harvard University Press.

Leibniz, Gottfried Willhelm, Freiherr von, 1689. "On Freedom", Philosophical Essays, Hackett Publishing Company, Inc.

Lucki, Irwin, Unpublished. Behavioral Models of Depression.

Mithen, S.J. 1996. The Prehistory of the Mind: A Search for the Origins of Art, Science and Religion. London & New York: Thames & Hudson.

Ryle, Gilbert, 1949. "Descartes' Myth", The Concept of Mind, University of Chicago Press.

Schank, Roger, 2000. Tell Me A Story. MacMillan Publishing

Searle, John, 1984. Minds, Brains, and Science, London : British Broadcasting

Smolensky, Paul, 1995. "Connectionism, Constituency, and the Language of Thought", Connectionism : debates on psychological explanation, volume two, edited by Cynthia Macdonald and Graham Macdonald, Cambridge , Mass. : Blackwell Publishers

Turing, Alan, 1950. "Computing Machinery and Intelligence", Mind Vol. 59, No. 236 (Oct., 1950), Oxford University Press.

Wegner, Daniel M., 2002. The Illusion of Conscious Will, The MIT Press.

Index

agent.. 58, *61*, 67, 73, 75, 96, *97*, 108, 112, 132, 141, 146, 147
Aleksander 82, 84, 158
Austen 76, 158
Automatic Modules 120
Baars . 118, 120, 121, 158
Carnap 31, *33*, *34*, *35*, 37, 38, 39, 40, 43, 45
Cartesian theater 131
causation *67*, 73, 112, 115, 123
Chalmers 78, 158
Chinese room .. 9, 13, 17, 85
connectionist ... 4, 22, 23, 24, 28, 88, 89, 90, 91
Consciousness ... 47, 77, 78, 80, 83, 95, 105, 109, 110, 140, 158, 160
Democritean 95

Dennett ... 63, 64, 95, 96, 97, 107, 108, 109, 110, 115, 124, *125*, 127, 129, 131, 135, 139, 147, 158
denotational 8, 15, 27
determinism .. *63*, 65, 66, 107
Dretske 4, 17, 19, 21, 23, 26, 29
Enderton 101, 158
Farah 158
Fellows 158
first-order logic. 102, 140
Fodor 4, 6, 8, 14, 16, 17, 25, 26, 30
Frankfurt. 55, *69*, 70, 71, 72, 73, 108, *125*, 159
Ginet 65, 70, 159
Gödel 101
Hall 75, 159
Hatfield.... 37, 39, 45
Hempel 159
higher order logics
.... 102

Hobbes 65, 159
Ideomotor 112
incompatibilist *65*
intentional stance . *97*
Intentionality 74
James Bond 130
Kane 66, 108, 160
Kuhn 136, 160
language of thought 5
Leibniz 126, 160
Libet 64, 109, 111, 160
Lucki 93, 160
Martin Luther 69
meaning' ... 5, 10, 19, 22, 26, 86
metarepresentation 19, 21, 24
mind-body problem 50
Mithen 98, 99, 160
Paradigm 135
performative utterance *76*
physicalism 31, *33*
possible worlds .. *124, 125, 126*
prefrontal cortex . 114
Principle of Alternative Possibilities 55, *69*, 159
protocol language 33

Quine ... 5, 16, 30, 95
Representational Theory of Mind 14
Ryle 50, 79, 160
Schank 113, 160
Schneider 30
Searle 3, 4, 5, 6, 7, 9, 10, 11, 12, 13, 15, 16, 17, 21, 26, 27, 30, 85, 87, 88, 101, 161
semantic 3, 6, 8, 9, 13, 14, 17, 26, 27, 87, 88, 91
Skinner 31, 37, 42, 45
Smolensky 4, 22, 23, 25, 26, 30, 89, 90, 91, 161
symbols . 4, 6, 10, 11, 14, 22, 26, 27, 86, 87, 88, 89, 91
syntax 4, 7, 9, 14, 21, 23, 27, 87, 88, 89, 90
system language .. *32, 33*
Tolman 31, *36*, 39, 43, 46
Turing . 6, 26, 85, 91, 116, 161

ventromedial prefrontal cortex 114
volition 54, *59*, *69*, 74, 117, 118, 137, 141

Volition **47**, *59*, 116, 141
Wegner 64, 109, 110, 111, 112, 128, 129, 130, 135, 161

www.ingramcontent.com/pod-product-compliance
Lightning Source LLC
Chambersburg PA
CBHW061649040426
42446CB00010B/1658